D1344328

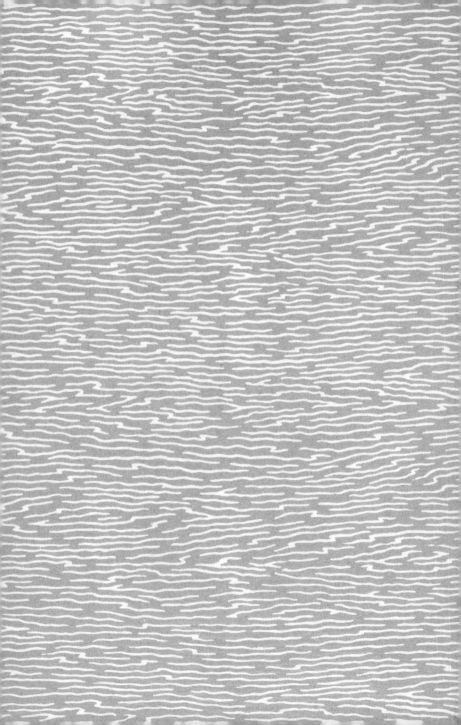

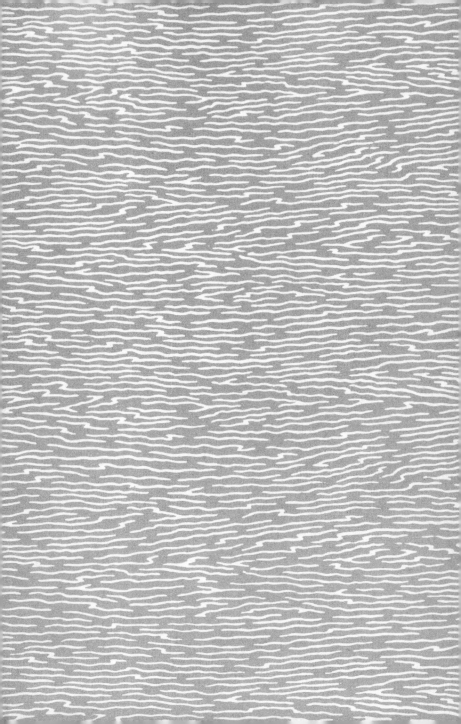

A NOTE ABOUT THE AUTHOR

Pico Iyer is the author of two novels and ten works of
nonfiction, translated into twenty-three languages. He
recently gave three TED Talks in three years, and they
have received more than eight million views so far.

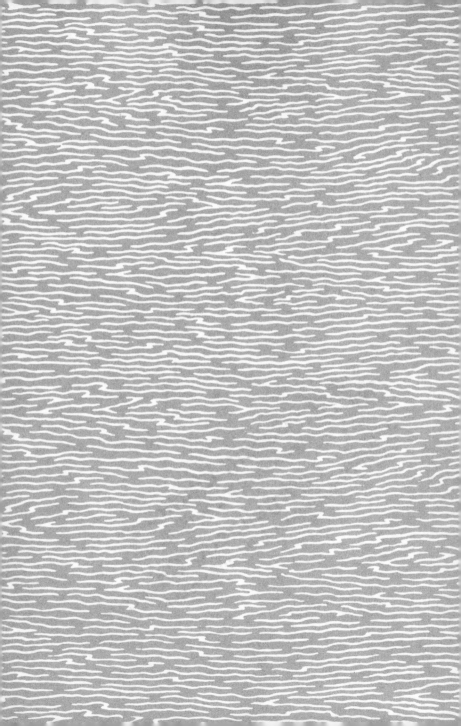

PICO IYER

AUTUMN
LIGHT

JAPAN'S SEASON OF
FIRE AND FAREWELLS

BLOOMSBURY PUBLISHING

LONDON · OXFORD · NEW YORK · NEW DELHI · SYDNEY

BLOOMSBURY PUBLISHING
Bloomsbury Publishing Plc
50 Bedford Square, London, WC1B 3DP, UK

BLOOMSBURY, BLOOMSBURY PUBLISHING and the
Bloomsbury Publishing logo are trademarks of Bloomsbury Publishing Plc

First published in 2019 in the United States by Alfred A. Knopf,
a division of Penguin Random House LLC, New York

First published in Great Britain 2019
This edition published 2020
Copyright © Pico Iyer, 2019

A catalogue record for this book is available from the British Library

ISBN: HB: 978-1-5266-1147-5; TPB: 978-1-5266-1148-2;
PB: 978-1-5266-1146-8; EBOOK: 978-1-5266-1149-9

2 4 6 8 10 9 7 5 3 1

Printed and bound in Great Britain by CPI Group (UK) Ltd,
Croydon CR0 4YY

To find out more about our authors and books visit www.bloomsbury.com
and sign up for our newsletters

In memory of Jikan, who showed me how to cherish the seasons inside us—and how to seek out changelessness in change

How happy
to see lightning
and not think, "Time is fleeting!"

—BASHO

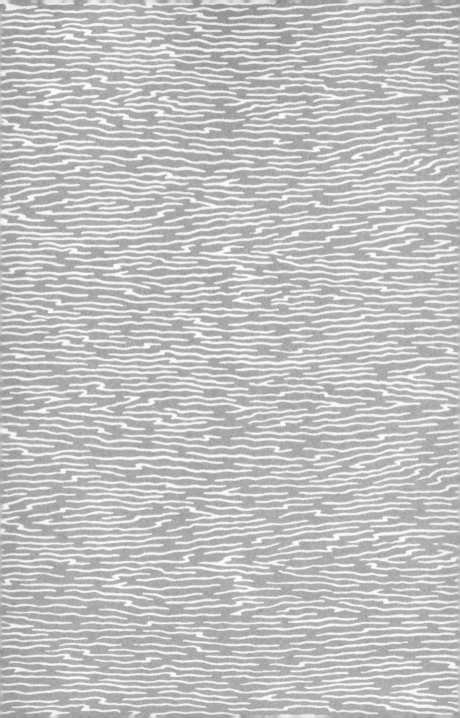

I

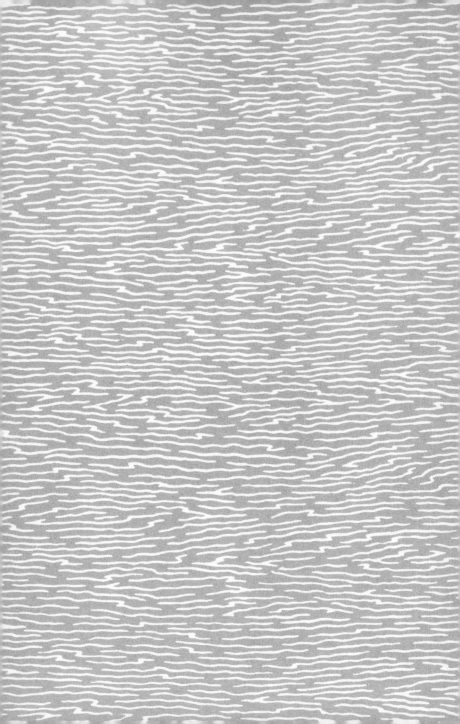

"*Tonight the crimson children are playing in the west,*" wrote Emily Dickinson in the fall of 1854, "*and tomorrow will be colder.*"

"I'm sorry." Hiroko's voice, made for singing, sounds flat, provisional.

"What is it?" Fumbling for the phone, I catch sight of the red digits on the hotel bedside table: 1:23.

"My father now hospital," says my wife, a dozen or more time zones away. "I'm sorry."

I try to clear my head. Drunks are reeling through the warm Florida night around me, taking me farther and farther away.

"What happened?"

"I don't know." I've never heard her so hesitant. "All white. Doctor say his blood all white."

"I'll be there soon," I say, though I know that words are useless when it comes to fear. I curse my job for taking me so far. In my mind's eye, I see my ultra-chic, motorbike-riding wife all but alone in a room of empty beds.

"It's difficult," she says again.

"But he came with you to the shrine last week? For a ritual visit?"

"I know," she says. There's another long pause. "They say, ninety-one years old, it can't be helped. Almost they don't care, he's so old."

"I'm sorry," I say again uselessly, almost Japanese. "I'll be there on Tuesday."

"No problem," she says. "It's difficult."

Two days later, the phone again—a bright Key West morning, all birdsong and sunlight.

"He's gone," says Hiroko, her brisk and efficient self again.

"I'm so sorry."

"It's okay. All night I hold his hand. Always together my father."

"Your mother?"

"Cannot understand."

"Maybe that's better?"

"Maybe." For years now, Hiroko's father, boyishly proud of his good health, has been tending to his beloved wife of sixty years, even as her mind and memory come slowly apart. Cycling to the shops to get their food. Heating up the green tea he chooses with such care as they gather on the tatami mat around a tiny table in their three-room wooden house. So caught up in his own concerns, he hasn't noticed—or chooses not to notice—that she's asking the same question again and again.

And then, bracing myself, I ask, "Your brother?"

"I don't know. I talk his wife."

Neither of us says a word. There's nothing to say. For twenty-three years, no one in the family has heard a thing from Masahiro, as I'll call him. We know he lives in a suburb of Kyoto, fifteen minutes from the creaking two-story structure where his parents stay. His office is in the same neighborhood as the elders' day-care center to which they've been taken three days a week for the past three years. But Hiroko's only sibling, a Jungian psychologist two years older than she, decided to sever all relations with his family soon after he returned from getting his doctorate in Europe. He's stuck to his resolve through sickness and typhoon.

"You're okay?" I ask Hiroko. "I'm so sorry I can't leave until Monday."

"Okay," says Hiroko, who seems to have emerged from a fog. "Now must make new life."

Masahiro's on my mind, he's all around me, as I rise from my bed a couple of return trips later. I'm sixteen hours out of sync following last night's flight, and when I draw back our thick gray curtains, I see just a few small white badges of light under a blue-ing sky. Hiroko is asleep in the only other room of our tiny rented flat—she's never lost the light sleep of a young mother—so I slip on T-shirt and jeans in the dark and shuffle into loafers in front of our gray door. The beaker of salt Hiroko placed outside our anonymous entrance purifies us all, I remember her saying, as I steal down two short flights of stairs in our three-story yellow apartment block, known as Lime Village.

Around me, the thin, straight, silent streets are empty. Most of the homes in our neighborhood, Deer's Slope, are Western-style, two-story, family dwellings, with tiny gardens out in front, the spotless lanes that run between them so narrow they lack even sidewalks. You can walk down any street here as if it were your own. Under a child's basketball net, a silver Mercedes dozes. Across the way, a midnight-blue Audi sits beside a chirpy sign advertising English lessons.

I hurry past the only house that takes up a full block, the place's gargoyles and silver cornices, its ornamental garden just visible behind the kindly old lady who sometimes pulls back the gate, marking it out as the haunt of a gangster. In the mini-park on the next block, I see a cartoon dog on a billboard smiling with relief as he scoops up his own poop.

When I arrive at the edge of the settlement, seven or eight minutes later, I can look across a valley of gray-tiled houses, a nine-family village, to the outline of hills far beyond.

Down the secret flight of stairs and through the middle of a mini-forest I hurry, to emerge in another century. A rambling two-story wooden house overlooks a persimmon tree and fields. The vegetable garden that Mr. Makihara from the ping-pong club tends in his autumn years is sprouting white radishes and lettuce. A giant emerald rice paddy in front of the pond looks like a vivid green hairbrush, overturned, bristles out.

The lane is so slim I'd have to press myself against a wall if a car came past. The speed limit here, a sign announces, is barely twelve miles per hour. I head up a steep slope and come to a stone torii gate, only a couple of feet taller than I am, slips of white paper fluttering from its top. Our closest place of worship—our modern neighborhood is cleansed of all shrines and temples—is named after Susano, the bad-boy god of waves and storms who was banished for smashing a hole in the hall of heaven belonging to his sister, the sun goddess.

I've never been a great one for belief, or for trying to put words to what's beyond us. Ten years in English boarding school was a lifelong training in skepticism, or at least in keeping to yourself anything you held sacred; every time I returned to my parents' yellow house on a hill in sixties California, the earnest, open faces of their students betrayed the poignancy of a longing for certainties. Yet, whenever I'm in the Deer's Slope post office, I thank the kindly woman who seeks out gorgeous stamps to affix to every postcard so that someone unknown to her in a distant land can enjoy a piece of Japan. I often tell the cheerful, head-scarfed matron in the Deer's Kitchen bakery how tasty her "hard bread" is. So it doesn't seem amiss to pay respects to the local spirits, who, Hiroko assures me, are the ones who ensure our health and long life.

A light comes on the second I walk across the darkened courtyard. I push a button with my foot next to the old stone basin in one corner, and cold water flows out of a dragon-headed spout. I pick up one of the blond wood ladles laid out on two rough boulders inside the basin and rinse my right hand, then my left. Then my mouth.

The shrine itself, a few steps away, is nothing but a rickety open-fronted wooden building behind a sign that says it's been here since 1575. Along the rafters are cracked paintings of scenes from classic plays, a yellowing portrait of a fresh-faced boy, faded depictions of the court, splinters of wood showing through the walls. Behind a barrier, keeping me from the cricket-chattering trees, two lion-dogs guard a wooden box, and ten stone lanterns—some with paper in their openings, some blank-eyed—protect a compact courtyard.

I pull the thick rope, clap my hands twice to summon the gods and close my eyes, hands joined. "Thank you," I think, "for looking after our home, and our family, this community, while I was gone. Thank you for protecting my mother and me in California. Thank you for keeping Hiroko safe. And her brother not so far."

Then, as the sun shows up above the hills, I turn around and begin to head back, through the silent village and up the stairs to our bright, rectilinear neighborhood of vending machines and hair salons. An old man is taking a walk through the sleeping streets—"Good morning," he calls, in the democracy of first light. In our central park, a square-block expanse across the street from our flat, the local dogs are gathering on the ridge for their daily 6:00 a.m. conference. The first executives, in suits, are lined up at the bus stop on the silent main drag, and Hiroko, I know, will soon be ringing her bell and sitting stock-still for twenty minutes in front of her homemade shrine before heading off, in black leather jacket and cat-cool shades, to her job selling overpriced English punk clothes in the temple town two train stations away.

Autumn is the season when everything falls away.

. . .

"Pico-san!"

I swivel round as I emerge from the elevator on the fifth floor at Renaissance, the local health club, fifteen minutes by foot up a hill, and see a cherubic badger in spectacles, buzz cut turning gray, barreling towards me, with a broad grin. Mayumi-san, as I'll call her, is a one-woman entertainment center; life is such constant delight for her that she fires out bulletins from some private sitcom, delivered at such high speed that even Hiroko cannot follow.

"Long time, no see, Pico-san. Where you been?"

Before I can stammer out a reply, she's casting an appraising glance at my T-shirt with the twenty-second-century blue robot cat on it, my Payless ShoeSource slip-ons with a hole in the sole, my battered expression.

"You look fat, Pico-san," she chuckles. "So old. Tired, too. What's with that?"

"I'm just off a plane. It's one in the morning in my stomach. Even later in my brain."

"You here for ping-pong?"

I nod. In the days when Mayumi-san was regularly part of our gathering, I often ended up, picking yarrow sticks, as her doubles partner. Before each serve, she whirled her arms around like a broken windmill and chuckled maniacally, "Here it comes, folks!" On the rare occasion when we won, she danced around with the abandon of a drunken bear, slapping my palms and flinging her arms around me in a crazed embrace.

"So, Pico-san, that your boyfriend?" She chortles as a very old man pads past, on his way home. He does not look amused.

My burly pal fills me in on the news, though at the speed of an old tape that's got snarled in fast-forward: Mrs. T. is still in hospital, and we seldom see her husband now, because he has to make the long trip out to take her home-cooked food every day; Mr. I. is not in evidence, because his wife expressed dissatisfaction at the fact that he devoted every spare evening and weekend minute to table tennis. Mayumi-san's eyes hurt, so she comes here only for the baths: no ping-pong for her now. But she sees me often, she reports, at the market, whenever she takes her grandkids for a walk.

More breaking news flies out, in local dialect, amidst a torrent of chuckles, and I just say, "Oh, really?"—happy at times to be limited in my Japanese.

Then she bundles off, an unstoppable force of self-amusement, to make mischief somewhere else. I walk down to the locker room, change quickly, and head up again, into the spotless, bare space marked "Studio."

There are four players at each of the three tables when I arrive, in front of the mirrored wall. Two different pairs are rallying at each table, across the diagonal, one pair hitting forehands to each other, very fast, the other backhands. Every now and then, the balls collide in midair, and everyone cries, "Waaah!"

Mrs. Fukushima, a tiny figure with short, waved dark hair, dressed as always in a pink shirt and long black slacks with thin pink stripes on them, comes up to me.

"Pico-san," she says in her soft, self-effacing voice, with a small smile. "Shall we?"

One pair pulls back from a table with a quiet word of invitation, and we take over. Our rallies begin slowly, but with each return, the ball starts flying over the net faster and faster, till, finally, our exchange concludes and Mrs. Fukushima begins giggling in shy delight, covering her mouth with her hand as she laughs.

When it's time for a game, my pale-faced, impassive adversary, barely five feet tall, stands where she is and blocks every shot, her paddle tilted at such a fiendish angle that the ball flies hard and fast over the net and nicks a corner, unanswerable.

I walk back to collect one of her lightning returns, and wonder whether I could ever have foreseen, in bright youth, that my ideal of an exhilarating Saturday night would one day involve hitting ping-pong balls to an eighty-three-year-old grandmother who says, so softly I can barely hear it, "I'm so glad I came today."

I long to be in Japan in the autumn. For much of the year, my job, reporting on foreign conflicts and globalism on a human scale, forces me out onto the road; and with my mother in her eighties, living alone in the hills of California, I need to be there much of the time, too. But I try each year to be back in Japan for the season of fire and farewells. Cherry blossoms, pretty and frothy as schoolgirls' giggles, are the face the country likes to present to the world, all pink and white eroticism; but it's the reddening of the maple leaves under a blaze of ceramic-blue skies that is the place's secret heart.

We cherish things, Japan has always known, precisely because they cannot last; it's their frailty that adds sweetness to their beauty. In the central literary text of the land, *The Tale of Genji*, the word for "impermanence" is used more than a thousand times, and bright, amorous Prince Genji is said to be "a handsomer man in sorrow than in happiness." Beauty, the foremost Jungian in Japan has observed, "is completed only if we accept the fact of death." Autumn poses the question we all have to live with: How to hold on to the things we love even though we know that we and they are dying. How to see the world as it is, yet find light within that truth.

This year, however, autumn's no mere decorative riddle. Four days after my father-in-law's death, I was back in Japan and taking a train to the station in southern Kyoto, just down the lane from the most important of all the land's twenty-two thousand harvest shrines, its ten thousand orange torii gates leading up and up a hillside of tiny statues and secret hollows. Posted alone outside the tiny wooden house where her parents had lived for five decades, Hiroko let me into the damp, stone-cold entrance hall, and led me up the short, winding staircase to two near-empty rooms.

In one, I saw a single bed, a chest of drawers; in the other, a bare tatami space and, within a dark corner, the household shrine, with a small framed photo of Hiroko's father on it, ghostly pale, the last time we took him for a drive. Behind him, a black-and-white picture of his longtime antagonist, his mother-in-law, severe in black kimono.

For thirty years or more, the gray shutters opening out onto the street rattled up every morning, and Hiroko's mother, in her worn apron, cat sleeping by her side, took her seat in front of a row of candies and soft drinks, to hand them out with smiles to passing kids and do a little business; behind her, in the bathroom-sized main room, her small, trim husband sat on a cushion on the floor, around a low table, taking care of accounts and sipping green tea, as horses clattered past on a small TV.

My father-in-law, in the Japanese way, had officially become a member of his wife's family after going into hospital in his thirties. "If anything should happen, will you protect my wife and kids?" he'd asked his own mother, and she, with characteristic briskness, always hungry for adventure, answered, "No." So he'd taken on the name of his wife's clan, and lived as a lone outlier from Hiroshima amidst wife and sister-in-law and mother-in-law, and all the constant whispers of a small, traditional Kyoto neighborhood.

Now, after all these years, there's almost nothing left in the tiny house. Hiroko shows me the albums of pre-digital photos her father used to keep under his pillow, of the one foreign holiday he took, when I brought him to California for five days. The images of Fisherman's Wharf and the beach at Carmel that he brought out to impress all who visited so they could say, "How great!" and hurry off. Next to the photos, the binoculars on which he'd emptied nearly all his savings, one hour after arrival, so he could take in the larger world he'd always dreamed of. Throughout the nine-hour flight, he'd never nodded off, lest he miss a special moment.

We gather a few supplies, and take a cab to the nursing home five minutes away where Hiroko's mother is now living: a tiny room, with one thin bed and a dresser on which sits a small framed picture of her late husband, cradling their two-year-old great-granddaughter.

I'm humbled by Hiroko's emotional efficiency; I wouldn't have had the courage to tell this eighty-five-year-old woman, who's just lost her husband and much of her mind, that she's now losing her home as well, for an anonymous cell. But if mother and daughter tried to share a space for even a month, we all know, neither would make it to the second week.

When we step into the small room, it's to find my mother-in-law gasping for breath, shoulders heaving up and down as she tries to catch some air. Hiroko bustles the old lady into sweater and socks, and, commandeering a wheelchair, steers her into an elevator and down into a waiting taxi. After we get out, ten minutes later, we might be entering a post-nuclear nightmare. In every chair in the large, bare entrance hall of the local hospital, a prospective patient is sitting in silence as red digits flash on screens above a broad desk. Hiroko parks her mother's wheelchair next to us, bundling the old lady up in blankets, and we await our turn.

Suddenly the old lady looks up. "Where's Grandpa?"

Since Hiroko's son and daughter came into the world, her parents have become "Grandpa" and "Grandma" to one and all.

"Is he at the races?"

"No, Grandma," my wife explains. "He died. Don't you remember? Last week he got pneumonia, and he had to go into the hospital."

"Ah yes," says the old woman. "He died. The tenth of the month. He always did love the races."

She returns to her silence, staring straight ahead of her, as other elderly souls are wheeled this way and that.

"So you and I are going to live alone?" she asks at last.

"No, Grandma," says Hiroko, struggling to keep calm. "I have a job in Nara, remember? If I don't work, we can't eat. You have a new home."

"So I live in the nursing home for life? I die in the nursing home? Alone?"

I reach for Hiroko's hand, as I see her struggling to stay afloat.

"You're not alone, Mother. You have me. You have your grandchildren. Don't you remember Soyo, your great-granddaughter?"

"What about Masahiro?" says her mother. "Maybe your brother will take me in, now you're refusing?"

"I don't know."

"I have two children," announces the old lady to all the world, shoulders rising and falling as she struggles to breathe, "and I have to live in a nursing home alone. Until I die."

. . .

"My heart goes out to your mother," I say to Hiroko as we head into the first of the three trains—followed by a bus—that take us home. I've suffered from asthma all my life; I know it's a strange compound of conditions in the world and conditions inside the heart.

"*Shikataganai!*" says Hiroko—it can't be helped. Though, the way she says it, so despairing, it sounds very much as if it can.

Her circumstances have been upended all but overnight, and she's responded to them with tremendous speed; but I notice there's no talk of selling the creaking building. A part of her must want to keep a piece of the past intact.

Our own home couldn't be more different from the wooden houses sticking out like crooked teeth among which my in-laws have been living, where the woman who sells flowers is talking about so-and-so's secret "second wife" around the corner, and the man in charge of fish is wondering what the policeman said to Morishita's little boy about the shoplifting. Our entire community, Deer's Slope, is laid out on a foreign model, like a stage set from the Universal Studios theme park a short subway ride away; a gray name-plaque gleams outside each discrete house, its front door six feet back from the street, and every Sunday I see men hosing down their German sedans to keep them as spotless as everything around them.

The two main axes of our ten-block grid, ruler-straight, are named Park-dori and School-dori, as if to assure my mostly retired, comfortable neighbors that they've achieved their life-time dream of migrating to a Japanese rendition of California. At the point where the axes meet, there's a short strip of mom-and-pop stores, to take care of daily necessities: a pharmacy, a photo salon, a bakery and, this being Japan, four beauty salons. At each of the three bus stops in the neighborhood is a large board that shows by family name every house in the vicinity.

If you're lost, though, you can always stop off at the police-men's shack, just next to the fire station, at the edge of the line of shops. Right across from it is the park, the village green that is the spiritual heart of our community, its line of maples and ginkgoes set out to project kaleidoscopic displays in late November, its avenue of cherries made for picnics as the blos-soms begin to froth in early April.

There used to be a sleek, two-story sports club overlooking the main park, like a fresh prop from *Close Encounters of the Third Kind*. It had an Easter Island statue outside one door, ivy climbing up its gray walls and, quite often, a red Ferrari parked in the lane outside. Now, however, the club is gone, and all that remains is the park with its coloring leaves and, down a little lane in one corner, a tearoom with an English name, Autumn.

A perfect reflection, in short, of the sleepy old city, Nara, of which Deer's Slope is a young suburb. For seventy-four years, in the eighth century, Nara was the first permanent Buddhist capital of Japan. Broad avenues were laid out on the model of Chang'an, then the capital of China, and a storehouse mark-ing its position as the last stop along the Silk Road came to be known as the world's first museum. Two and a half million people worked on constructing a central temple, Todaiji—or so the temple's administrators claim—and for twelve centuries it was the largest wooden building on the planet; inside is what remains the largest bronze sculpture in the world, a five-hundred-tonne, forty-nine-foot Buddha. A twelve-minute train ride brings you to the oldest wooden building in the world, and all around are the plains on which it's believed the sun goddess gave birth to imperial Japan, six centuries before the birth of Christ.

Yet what I love most about Nara is its neglectedness, a slightly forlorn quality that makes it almost a monument to autumn. Only three generations after the capital came up in Nara, the court moved to the outskirts of Kyoto, twenty miles to the north, and it was Kyoto, capital for the next 1178 years, that became the center of geisha culture, of Zen temples, of flower arrangement and garden design and kimono. More recently, it's supple, worldly-wise Kyoto that gave birth to the Super Mario Bros., to Haruki Murakami, to the Nobel Prize–winning scientist who helped invent blue LED lights. Hiroko's hometown is a silky courtesan who knows how to bewitch every newcomer, even in old age, with her natural sense of style, her lacquered designs; Nara is the absentminded older brother who's forever pottering around in his garden, wondering where he put the key.

Whenever I consult a map from the tourist office in central Nara, I delight in the large empty swatches marked out in English as "ancient burial mounds" or "primeval forest." There was once a single eight-screen cinema in central Nara, but it got torn down. There was once a single department store, but

it closed its doors. So, too, for a while, the only Starbucks outlet. As in some fairy tale, the very heart of this city of 350,000
consists of the largest municipal park in Japan, through which
roam twelve hundred wild deer. A white deer is said to have
been seen carrying a Shinto god over the hills here in the year
763, and when the word arrived that the Buddha had delivered
his first discourse in a deer park, the creatures' status as "god
messengers" was confirmed.

Go to the five-story glass-and-concrete prefectural office
on Nara's wide main drag and you're greeted by three ant-
lered stags sitting serenely outside the front door. Walk out
of the two-story wooden Nara Hotel, where one of Tanizaki's
Makioka sisters encountered bedbugs, and you're less likely to
see doormen than soft-eyed does. It's hard not to feel that the
deer, and in fact the whole spirit-filled realm they represent,
are still the true rulers of this rustic town.

At the time I arrived in Japan, in 1987, when the ten largest
banks in the world were all Japanese, the government decided
that it could now design the planetary future. Where better,
it was decided, to base this bold Tomorrowland than in the
proud, ancestral heart of old Japan, where even the train stations use the ancient name for Japan, Yamato, to invoke its tal-
ismanic magic? Very quickly, groves of cedar and cypress said
to be thick with water spirits, and mountains so sacred humans
could not set foot on them, began to sprout a national library
with rainbow slats, futuristic research centers and pieces of
concrete origami befitting a Mountain View East. Every time I
walk away from Susano Shrine, near our home, along a patch
of trees, I come, within ten seconds, to a view of a nine-story

glass structure that reflects back a giant mosaic of Albert Einstein sticking out his tongue. Across the street is an R-and-D center shaped like a retina.

But six years after Japanese bought Rockefeller Center in Midtown Manhattan—suddenly the complex that contained my office was Japanese—they had to sell it again, for half the price they had paid. So now, when I walk around our neighborhood, it's to see the sci-fi cathedrals of tomorrow sitting abandoned along their empty highways, their parking lots empty, their ornamental ponds quite dry. Kyoto is said to be the most visited city in the world outside of Mecca, drawing fifty-five million visitors a year to its Golden Temple and Philosopher's Path, its Parisian cafés and International Manga Museum; when I walk around Nara after dark, all I can see are dim lanterns, and deer stepping between the trees.

Balls are flying across six tables as I step into the ancient yellow-walled gym where the Deer's Slope Ping-Pong Club meets for maverick games on Saturday afternoons, the one day we don't go to the health club. Mr. Joy, as I've named him in my head, is standing eight feet behind the table and delivering his fast, looping forehand topspins, again and again, at a tiny woman in her fifties, who is smashing efficiently back. A bespectacled man using a dull-gray towel as a bandanna is chopping back slams with practiced ease as another old gent, with a grizzled army cut, flips balls back at high speed.

Many of the older men use the "penholder" grip associated with China, clutching their sanded-off bats between their fingers as if wielding chopsticks and turning themselves into human spaghetti to hit a backhand with the same side of the bat they use for forehands. The rest of us deploy the Western "shake hands" grip that I learned, almost fifty years ago, from an enigmatic Chinese sage in California who presented himself as "Gene" (or was it "Djinn"?) Lee.

I think of the games I used to play as a boy, alone in our solitary house, halfway up the hills in Santa Barbara, flipping one side of the table up so that it hit my every slam back with the speed and wizardly angles of Mrs. Fukushima. At the Dragon School in Oxford, ping-pong was how I and my equally tiny friend, Peter, tried to show we weren't completely hopeless in the only thing that counted—games—and at high school and even graduate school, it became the way I escaped from reading *Beowulf* yet again and reciting Greek irregular verbs, and slipped back into carefree boyishness.

Now, as I look around me, at these neighbors older than my uncles and aunts, everything is upended: a reminder that Japan has the oldest population in the world—more diapers are sold to the elderly here than to babies—and a vision of how the characters around me are twirling the seasons around like dance partners.

Outside, in the sun, kids are clambering across a huge-masted Spanish galleon in the compact park, while little brothers swing blue baseball bats at the softballs their fathers throw at them. Tiny girls are squealing their way down the chutes of an elaborate pink contraption that resembles nothing so much as a melted Dalí sand castle. Soon the trees will be flaming red and gold all around them—I'll catch something of the vivid symphony through the door in the gym, the second-floor windows—and then my friends and I, in the dark days of winter, will find ourselves playing in mufflers and jackets, clutching paddles through mittens and unable to sit down as our hands grow numb as baseball mitts.

Around me inside the gym, the furious shouts of twelve young female volleyballers, in tight ponytails, playing nine against three on the far side of the old basketball court, drown out our mild-mannered club boss as he summons our group for the day's announcements.

I'm the only one—foreigner's prerogative—who skips the first seventy-five minutes of every session, starting with group calisthenics and informal pep talk, then turning into hour-long practice drills. Instead I arrive, straight from my desk and perturbingly fresh, halfway through the afternoon, just as the actual games begin. Very soon, however, I'm the only one sweating, hands on my thighs as I catch my breath, while the unrelenting chorus rises up around me. "Pico-san, what's up? You're the youngest by far, and you're the first to get tired?"

"*¡Hola!*" cries Noguchi-san now, coming up to shake my hand and grinning under his tousled white hair. He still listens to the radio for fifteen minutes every morning to master Spanish, but, so far as I can tell, they teach the same few words every week. He speaks pretty good English from his three years in Pattaya in the 1970s, helping to build one of the first beach hotels in Thailand, but for some reason—I'm no better, in Japanese—he specializes in asking questions in a language he can't begin to follow the answers to.

"How's Silvia?" I say, trying to rescue us from an unending exchange of *"¿Como está?"*s.

"Oh, you're clever," laughs my skinny, bronzed old friend. "You remember!"

How could I forget? He'd named his golden retriever after a beautiful girl he'd seen, thirty years ago, in a village in the Philippines. He'd love to go back to Thailand or the Philippines, but the seventy dollars a day it would take to house aging Silvia at a pet hotel makes the prospect difficult.

The women in the group are busy handing around halftime snacks, and a kindly matron in a purple T-shirt that says "I Believe in Love" presses a second ice cream on a large, chuckling man with a kind, soft face.

"Izumi-san," she says, "you should take this. You're the biggest one here."

"How big are you, anyway?" one of the men teases. "Eighty kilos?"

"Naw," says another, as poor Izumi-san shyly collects the chocolate-chip ice-cream bar. "His head alone must weigh thirty kilos."

We pick yarrow sticks with black numbers inscribed on their bottoms to select doubles teams, and then, as pairs assemble on each side of every table, scissors cut my paper and someone on the other side of the table elects to serve. A man pulls out from a string bag a three-star ball, much heavier and more professional than our "training balls," and guaranteed to make each game a misery: since every table uses just one ball, we have to race across the gym to fetch it after every slam, slithering around someone at one of the other five tables who is preparing for a topspin drive, even slipping under the green net that separates us from the volleyballers if our ball begins to roll across the floor where a tall young girl is rising for a spike.

When the two-set games are finished, after an hour of high-speed doubles, everyone changing teams every eight minutes or so, and nobody aware of having lost, it's Ms. Teraki, as ever, who comes up to ask me if I'd like to hit a few. She's always friendly to the point of flirtiness, pert in her fresh red lipstick and bowl of dark hair, tiny as a third-grader, yet smashing forehands and backhands with the long, swaggering strokes of a man. When I hand her my three hundred yen—it's her turn this month to be club treasurer—she wraps my hand in her own warm palm as she gives me change.

We stand behind the table and swap long, arcing topspins—she goes for a slam on every shot—and every now and then my brisk and never-tiring friend lets out a high-pitched squeal and flashes a girly smile.

Not long ago, I asked her, as Japanese protocol encourages, how old she was, and heard, "Seventy-two."

"Not possible," I said, and meant it; she hit me on the arm with a coquettish bat.

"He's a writer," Teraki-san is saying now, almost with pride, as a newcomer, covering her mouth with her paddle, asks what's up with the scruffy hooligan with the peeling rubber paddle. "He lives in Deer's Slope, with his wife. Japanese, very cute. But his mother is in California. He's a journalist. *New York Times*." She's taking some liberties, but I'm amused she doesn't pass on the nickname I once heard the neighborhood kids use for me: "Isoro," or "Parasite." No surprise: I'm the only male in the neighborhood who doesn't put on suit and tie and go out to the bus stop every morning before dawn; even worse, I send my wife out, while I slouch around the neighborhood unshaven, close to lunchtime.

Our club chair, wordless and imperturbable in his dark-blue warm-up jacket with flashes of yellow lightning across it, sits out a game so others can play. Every now and then he intervenes to rearrange couples who seem to be mismatched, pairing this shy matron with that chubby grandfather who's just her level. Quite a few of the women sit on gray folding chairs against the wall and chat; the men, more silent, give themselves over to ferocious, intense rallies, flinging themselves to the floor to return a spinning forehand.

"Well, Pico-san," says tiny Mrs. Fukushima as she shuffles past, holding what might almost be a lacrosse stick, to pick up loose balls across the gym. At eighty-three, she's scooping up balls for the rest of us as if she were one of the teenage girls on the volleyball court.

"You aren't tired?" I ask, as she takes the table for another game, standing in place as she prepares to tilt her bat at mathematical angles.

"Oh no," she laughs back, moving an inch to block my fast topspin drive with a paddle so craftily bent that the ball tickles the far side of the table before flying away.

"I'm not tired, because I never move."

. . .

It was in autumn that I first got upended by Japan, and realized that not to live here would be to commit myself to a kind of exile for life. I was returning, at the age of twenty-six, to my office in New York City from a business trip to Hong Kong, all high-rising boardrooms and banquets in the casinos of Macao, and my Japan Airlines itinerary called for an overnight layover at Narita Airport, near Tokyo. It was the last thing I wanted; Narita was infamous for eleven years of violent protests by local farmers over the demolition of their rice paddies, culminating in a burning truck sent through the new airport gates not many years before. But I couldn't argue with flight schedules, and soon I was walking through the high-tech quiet of the arrivals area, and out into a singing autumn afternoon.

A shuttle bus took me to an airport hotel, and an elevator carried me up to my floor. When I got out, the long corridor was so spotless that all I could see was the window at the far end, framing the first crimson and gold from the surrounding trees. It was hard to tell where the forest ended and the building began.

After breakfast next morning, I still had four hours to kill before check-in, so I followed a sign in the lobby to a free shuttle van into the airport town. Twenty minutes later, I was dropped off on a busy road and crossed a street to find myself in a world suddenly intimate and human-scaled. The streets were barely wide enough for cars here, and many of the houses were made of wood. Paneled doors were pulled back, and, above the tatami mats of tearooms and restaurants, I could see, again, trees beginning to turn, through the picture windows at their back. Everything was silent, deserted, and the mildness of the late-October sky gave a sense of brightness and elegy to the day.

I followed the riddle of streets up to a large gate, which led into a courtyard thick with sweet incense. At the far end sat a wide wooden meditation hall, and all around stood protective statues and what looked to be graves. I didn't know then that Narita was a celebrated pilgrimage site, consecrated to the god of fire, or that people were known to walk the forty-six miles from central Tokyo to pay homage to its thousand years of history; I had no intimation that the Dalai Lama would be visiting months later, and sent his monks here to gain familiarity with the Shingon sect of Buddhism, the esoteric, mystical Japanese school closest to his own.

I simply followed random impulse out into the temple's garden, where a flock of kindergartners, in pink and blue caps, was scattering across the lawns, collecting fallen leaves. And almost instantly, for no reason I could fathom, I felt I knew the place, better than I knew my apartment in New York City, or the street where I'd grown up. Or maybe it was the feeling I recognized, the mingled pang of wistfulness and buoyancy.

I was so affected—the quiet morning went through me so deeply—that by the time I boarded my plane in early afternoon, I'd decided to leave my comfortable-seeming job in New York City and move to Japan. Four autumns later, I arrived, suitcase in hand, outside the door of a tiny temple along the eastern hills of Kyoto. My boyish plan was to spend a year in a bare room, learning about everything I couldn't see in Midtown Manhattan.

That idea lasted precisely a week, which was long enough for me to realize that scrubbing floors and raking leaves before joining two monks crashed out in front of the TV was not quite what my romantic notions had conceived. So I moved to an even smaller room, seventy-five square feet—no toilet, no telephone, no visible bed—and told myself that in the margins of the world was more room to get lost and come upon fresh inspiration.

Better still, I was back to basics here, with few words to support me and no contacts; my business card and résumé, liberatingly, meant nothing in Japan. Every trip to the grocery store brought some wild surprise, and I barely thought to look at my watch, every day seemed to have so many hours inside it. When, on my third week in the city, I went to Tofukuji, one of Kyoto's five main centers of Zen, to observe its abbot, Keido Fukushima-roshi, receive initiation into some new level of responsibility, I was placed next to a spirited and charming young mother of two from southern Kyoto whose name was Hiroko. She invited me to her daughter's fifth-birthday party, five days later, and very soon my year of exploring temple life became a year of watching a new love take flight.

Now, as I step into the post office in Deer's Slope, I can hardly recall the bright-eyed kid who made such a pious point of telling himself that purity and kindness and mystery lay inside the temple walls and that everything outside them was profane; the beauty of Japan is to cut through all such divisions, and to remind you that any true grace or compassion is as evident in the convenience store—or at the ping-pong table—as in the bar where two monks are getting heartily drunk over another Hanshin Tigers game.

My trusty protector behind the post-office counter, black waved hair down to her shoulders, flashes me a smile of welcome, and I allow myself to imagine she might be glad of a break after a morning of handling family pension matters. I place the kimono I'm sending to a ten-year-old goddaughter in London on her scales and, long familiar with my clumsiness, she offers to box it up and asks if the little girl would enjoy some pictures of Nara deer on the package. The one time, fatally, I came in during the designated Pico-handler's lunch break, a much younger woman collected my postcard as if it might be infectious, asked if Singapore was in Europe, hurried back to whisper frantic questions at the coffin-faced boss near the door and ended up charging me four dollars for a stamp.

Now, after buying a 3-D postcard of two bears enjoying green tea in kimono—my mother never can resist such zany pieces of Japan—I head out into the little lane of shops, past the computer store that once placed two white kittens in its windows to attract customers. In the local supermarket, the quiet, pale lady with the sad Vermeer face and braids running down to her waist looks relieved that, for once, I haven't left a copy of Henry Miller effusions in the photocopy machine. An old man is sitting alone at a small table next to where the mothers are briskly boxing up their groceries, as if waiting for a bridge game to begin. Across the street, the fountain of good cheer at the bakery is bustling around to slice fresh loaves as a soft-voiced woman purrs on the FM station.

Our main park begins less than two hundred yards behind the shops, and as I pass the elementary school, I can hear kids chanting, this warm blue day, the forty-seven syllables of the hiragana alphabet, in the ceremonial song that features every syllable once and once only.

A little like the Anglican hymns we used to sing in school, I think—or the Pledge of Allegiance, which we had to shout out during my brief time in a California classroom.

This song, though, might be the scripture of Japan. "Bright though they are in color, blossoms fall," I hear the children shouting out. "Which of us escapes the world of change? We cross the farthest limits of our destiny, and let foolish dreams and illusions all be gone."

I'd never lived by a farmer's calendar until I arrived in Deer's Slope, and it was hard for me to guess that even the Disney-worthy Californian houses along School-dori could be guided by a cycle of nine harvests and petitions to the sun goddess. Last autumn, Hiroko and I went to spend two nights on Mount Koya, the mountain of Shingon temples two hours from our home, and watched monks carrying fresh breakfast and lunch every day through the forest to the founder of the temples, Kobo Daishi, who "passed into deepest meditation" in the year 835. In Ise, two hours in another direction, I'd seen similar meals transported twice a day to the empty space that houses, so it's believed, the sun goddess. There are sixteen phases of the moon here—I try never to confuse the "waiting moon" with the "waiting for the twilight" moon—and I'm sometimes reminded that, as in classical China, there are seventy-two seasons in the year, so that every five days marks a new old world.

"Soon must eat rice cake," Hiroko had said yesterday, pulling out her compact diary, adorned with pictures of Peter Rabbit, and showing me that the harvest moon, said to be so bright that farmers can continue working after dark, will be visiting a few days from now; little boys will race around a pond in central Nara, carrying white globe lanterns with rabbits on them—there's a rabbit, not a man, on the moon in Japan—while a bamboo flute stabs notes out into the night. I never forget the year I showed up to find a completely empty setting, nothing but silhouettes of temples all around, and, realizing I'd got the day wrong, had to walk down nearby shopping streets to a screening of *Rush Hour 3* in an equally deserted cinema.

My neighbors all bow before the seasons here, as before the larger forces that keep us in our place. And autumn is at least more radiant, and a little less abrupt, than the earthquake that set off three hundred fires in Kobe, thirty miles away, not long after we moved here, or the tsunami two years ago that swept more than eighteen thousand people away to their deaths. The season is a kind of religion, I think, to which we offer poems and petitions, but it's not one you believe in so much as simply inhabit.

Very soon, there'll be tangy apples in the supermarket, replacing watermelons, and they'll bear the kinds of names that Thoreau relished as the trees turned apple-red around him: the Truant's Apple, the Saunterer's Apple, Wine of New

England, the Beauty of the Air. A little later, tiny, sweet tangerines will appear, the kind my father-in-law used to send me every year from a special farm in his beloved Hiroshima.

It took me a while, after I settled down here, to realize that every detail—the apples, the boxes they sit in, the table on which we place them—counts, because none of these things is inanimate in Japan. Only yesterday, Hiroko remembered, "I small time, I kicking table—sometimes little angry—every time, my father say, 'You must apologize! To table. That table has heart. It never hit you. Why you must hit it?'"

If she threw a pencil across the room, she was told, she might have been flinging her older brother against a wall.

When my mother-in-law was born, there was a deity on the throne, direct descendant of the sun goddess; but after the Emperor was pronounced a mortal, it was other forces that the people of Japan could more dependably rely upon, the "eight million gods" of rice paddy and wind, maple tree and constantly changing sky, whose presence we can never forget.

As my second autumn in Japan came to an end, twenty-five years ago, I had to return to California, in part because I'd promised a book to my publisher; but I could no more take leave of the place than I could of Hiroko, or of the world she'd opened up to me. I started pitching ideas for pieces that would bring me back to Kyoto, or finding assignments that would take me to Thailand, when Hiroko could free herself up to join me there. A little like Japan itself in its postwar decades, we'd stumbled out of the lives we'd planned, with nothing definite to step into.

In the book I published, I took pains to make its ending wistful and ambiguous, Japanese; Hiroko and I were eager—of course—there be no ending at all, but by then she had drawn me deeply enough into her culture that I couldn't believe any emotion could be unmixed, and I could see how sadness often lasts longer than mere pleasure. Endings seemed like sanctuaries in which humans hid to protect themselves from a larger, wilder landscape, and it hardly mattered to me whether they were happy or sorrowful, since the story kept unfolding.

Hiroko, in the meantime, had walked out of her marriage and taken her kids off to a tiny apartment one train station away from where they'd been. Her closest American friend was living alone with two kids in Kyoto, teaching English and studying Zen; why, she thought, could not a Japanese woman do the same? A divorce was heresy in Japan in those days—an act of failure on the woman's part, a rent in the country's woven tapestry—but, as more and more Japanese women began to be exposed to foreign lives, such separations became quite common.

Once more, it seemed, she was taking her prompt from the visitors she met; if we could travel far from home, and live quite happily, why could not she as well? And soon this small woman who'd never been on a plane a year before—barely stepped outside Kyoto—was leading equally bewildered Japanese everywhere from Hong Kong to Bangkok.

But a life of adventure doesn't go easily with raising kids, so, finally, she took a job near Kyoto Station, at an English-language school, and then, two autumns later, she found a very small apartment in Deer's Slope, ninety minutes away from her former life, but, conveniently, only three efficient train rides from where her parents and old friends were.

"Maybe you little try?" she said to me during one of our daily long-distance phone calls, and I could see that it was time. My parents' house in California, where I'd been staying, had burned to the ground in a forest fire, leaving me with nothing but the clothes I was wearing, and after five years of knowing Hiroko and her children, it hardly seemed too early to shelve my boy's fantasies of the writing life and move in, devoting my days to sending the kids through school.

Now, as I leave the two-room space that has been home for more than twenty years, I watch the office girls pull the straps of their dresses straight as they hasten to the bus stop a few yards away from our flat. Boys are playing catch outside the small wooden shack plastered with posters on environmental issues and unfair trade agreements that Hiroko calls "little Red group world." I think of how, just days after I came back this month, we marked a seventh-century holiday instituted for respecting the aged, a practice that cuts ever deeper as the years flip past.

On two sides of Deer's Slope are plunging valleys, one of which is entirely empty, the other of which leads to Susano Shrine; on a third side is a small hill, at the foot of which sit large bulldozers, ready to turn wilderness into profit. The fourth side opens out onto the normal, less gated world of coffee shops and convenience stores and the next suburb along,

Slope of Light. There was once a small convenience store in Deer's Slope, ten seconds from our flat. But then our neighbors noticed that it was a magnet for restless teenagers, and it went the way of the little cross on the second floor of the drab apartment building above the convenience store that marked the "Baptist Church."

My friends in the West sometimes ask if Japan isn't crowded, and I can't always explain how a people used to living together in a small space have grown so adept at self-containment—even at self-erasure—that our two-room apartment, when four people slept here, felt larger than my mother's five-bedroom home in the hills of California. What makes the air feel thronged is the presence of household deities and ghosts, the spirits that for my neighbors inhabit every last desk or box of chocolates. Nothing essential ever seems to die in Japan, so the land is saturated with dead ancestors, river gods, the heavenly bodies to whom Hiroko gives honorifics, as if they were her country's CEOs.

This morning, as I'd called out, "Would you like some tea?" Hiroko had shouted back, "Please give some my father."

I know better than to say a word. Every day at first light, she heats up food and boils his favorite tea to place in front of her improvised shrine, before getting herself up in tight ponytail and Italian short coat and grabbing the *American Idiot* CD from the boom box next to the shrine to serenade her on the way to work.

Today, when she got up, she hurried off for a shower. Then, on emerging, she started scrambling around the room at very high speed, sweeping up every piece of scrap paper, stuffing sunglasses and iPhone and lipstick into her Michael Kors bag, then hastening to the door.

"Isn't it your day off?" I called from the desk. The flat is so small, we're effectively in the same room wherever we are.

"Day off," she called back. "You no remember? O-Higan."

I don't remember. I never do. On the autumn equinox—today—the sun sets in exactly the western area where the Japanese believe their paradise to be; divisions between the living and the dead are porous.

"I little go visit my grandma," she says, wriggling into her short black boots and then heading off, for a two-hour, four-train trip in each direction, as if forgetting there's now another presence in the plot of graves, her father's.

It's hard to say what separates her grandmother from the Buddha. The picture of the deceased old lady has stood on the shrine in the wooden house in Kyoto ever since my first visit, and it's her maxims I hear more often than those of any sutra. In Hiroko's stories, her mother's mother sat above the daily family squabbles like a kind of household god, administering justice even as she was impassively stitching the group together. When Hiroko closes her eyes and prays for my good health, she might be praying to her grandmother as much as to any religious figure.

At the end of the war, the old woman, who had lost her husband years before, was effectively stripped by the Occupation government of the one hundred houses she owned in Osaka. So she decided to move to Kyoto to buy a little wooden structure near the most central fox shrine in the land, and set it up as a place for selling cigarettes and candies. When, soon after her arrival, a minor mobster arrived on her doorstep to demand protection money, the stocky lady stepped out and said, "Show me your boss! I'm not going to deal with some tiny hoodlum like you!" She never got bothered again.

After Hiroko returns this evening from the long trip—cleaning the headstone, sweeping the area around the grave free of debris, bringing in more buckets of water in case the old woman is thirsty—I ask her how it went.

"I so happy talk my grandma," she says. "Little Takeuchi family newspaper."

"What was the news?"

"My mother okay. My aunt okay. My children fine. My brother okay, I think, but we don't know."

"Your grandmother was close to him?"

"So close. Always he her favorite. My grandma little introduce candy, I always want more, more. Too greedy! She not so like me. My cousin little princess feeling. But everyone love my brother."

Decent, steady, high-achieving: he sounds like the solid pillar in a hurricane.

"But when she was old . . ."

"I always together her. My brother in Kansas that time, so far. My cousin very busy." Hiroko always gets on best with people when they're broken, their needs clearly visible. "She watching my husband, she little think my brother."

"And by the time your brother returned . . ."

"She gone. He so upset. Even he marry, he thinking Grandma."

"He wanted her approval?"

"Different! He choose wife because she same Grandma."

I'm lost, as ever; his bride was in her late twenties then, and her similarity to an elderly grandmother would not, I think, have been the greatest of her attractions.

But Hiroko assures me that her grandmother, apart from arranging her parents' marriage, was the force behind her brother's wedding, too. And now that her sister-in-law has put on some weight . . . well, she does look a lot like her husband's grandmother.

"Sorry," Hiroko says abruptly, "I must erase." She hurries to the bathroom, pulls out the bucket of salt under the sink, and scatters it all around. I'd forgotten that every trip to a grave must be annulled through purifying salt.

Then she showers and changes her clothes, to remove all scent of the dead. She's back in the fresh white shirt and jeans of the living.

From outside, we can hear a ball being thrown against a wall, again and again, as the sky turns dark blue and the night begins to chill.

The light is streaming through our windows this morning before the hands on my clock are upright, for 6:00 a.m. I look at Hiroko, and we know: summer's gone. Gone the ceaseless, seething buzz of crickets in the park, making the whole place seem to buzz and thrum; gone the shuttlecock rain of late afternoon that carries us in a moment into the tropics during the rainy season. I look out the window, and see no women cycling around in black elbow-length gloves and Darth Vader visors to keep the sun at bay; the old men who walk around the neighborhood in groups of four or five, green armbands around their elbows as they clean up every windblown piece of trash or rescue children who've gotten lost, no longer flap about like soggy ducks in flip-flops or baggy trousers, pulling out hand towels to mop their brows.

Summer is the impossible season in Japan; news programs report how railway lines nearby have warped in the heat, after eleven straight days of three-digit temperatures, and in the shadeless spaces and temples, there's nowhere to turn as the sun goddess reminds us of who's boss. Summer is also, para-doxically, the season of death: I flew back this year from a brief trip to Kashmir, and stepped out of a clamor of soldiers and roadblocks into the central event of midsummer Japan, Obon. For three days in mid-August, it's believed, the dead return to their homes, to look in on their loved ones, and the whole country stops while people scatter to their ancestral places to welcome back the ghosts.

In our case, the ceremonials were hardly impersonal; we'd lost someone close to us this year. On the last day of Obon, our son, Takashi, with his wife and two-year-old, comes down from Yokohama, 220 miles away, and Hiroko's cousin, an almost-sister from around the corner, shows up, with her nine-year-old son and aged mother and father. Our daugh-ter, Sachi, joins us, too, in the tiny upstairs bedroom in the little wooden house near the train tracks. In the middle of the empty tatami room where sits the family shrine, my mother-in-law has arranged herself on a cushion on the floor, next to her departed husband and her mother.

In the countryside, villagers are carving cucumbers in the shape of horses, to urge their ancestors to return for the Festival of the Dead as speedily as possible; they'll make oxen out of eggplants, to send them back to the heavens at a slower pace. Bonfires are lit outside homes so that none of the specters will lose their way. In Kyoto, a lantern appears next to each of the gravestones in the Otani Cemetery, overlooking the busy streets of downtown; twenty thousand lights come on at dusk, wavering above the neon and streaking cars of the geisha district.

When Hiroko and I walked along the broad white gravel pathway last night—the nearby bells rang out, "Everyone soon die," as Hiroko translated, "Do something now!"—we found the huge medieval gates to the "city of tomorrow," as a cemetery in Japan is called, pulled back. Beside them was a large white board on which bold strokes of calligraphy had been scrawled in black. "We may have radiant faces in the morning," read the translation into English, "but in the evening are no more than white bones."

Now, as the buzzer goes off in the little house, Hiroko flies down the stairs and returns with a cheerful priest, as brisk as an insurance salesman in his gray crew cut, even as his purple-and-green robes billow around him. Almost no one had laid eyes upon this man this time a year ago; but as soon as my father-in-law died, Hiroko was obliged to track down the temple with which the family is associated. The priest appeared and sold her a headstone for ten thousand dollars. He offered her a special Buddhist name to protect her father in the after-world for another thousand dollars (I questioned this, and she protested, "Very special name is two thousand!"). And on the seventh day after the death, the forty-ninth, the hundredth—for years into the future—he will appear and chant the Heart Sutra at high speed: "No old age and no death; no end to age and death; no suffering, nor any cause of suffering, nor end to suffering; no path, no wisdom."

Now the ceremonial figure settles in on the tatami mat in the bright morning sunshine, in front of the shrine, and delivers, so fast as to be almost incomprehensible, the unflinching verses, the roar of a passing train drowning him out every now and then. My father-in-law was always impatient with such rites, but I can see how they offer a container for grief, a time-tested way of channeling sorrow so that every family can be joined with every other. The big question after any death is "What now? And what will I do with this confusion and rage?" Perhaps the by-the-book rites offer a release?

As soon as he's finished, the priest accepts a cup of green tea and makes small talk, in the way of a country vicar. "So," he tells Hiroko's mother, "your son is now the head of the family."

He catches the unsettled glances all around and says, "No, no. I mean your grandson."

The prodigal son is fifteen minutes away, presumably celebrating the Festival of the Dead alone, with his wife and two daughters.

Then—there must be many deaths to mark—the priest makes his apologies and bustles off to his car downstairs. Across the hills of Kyoto tonight, five bonfires will be lit—one in the shape of a gateway to a shrine, another to represent a boat—as the departed leave the earth again.

Hiroko's mother looks around, startled.

"Where's Grandpa?"

"He's here, Grandma," says Hiroko. "But not exactly here." She points to the small photo on the shrine. "That's why everyone's come today."

"Ah yes," says the old lady, with an apologetic chuckle. "He died. On the tenth. He never would have wanted to miss an occasion like this."

She seems as cordial and full of wrinkled smiles as ever— the days of widowhood are accumulating—but underneath that is something that hasn't forgotten at all where she is. After lunch, we take her to a hospital, to which she's been committed, because the nursing-home staff can no longer get her to eat.

As soon as she's back in her thin bed in a room full of beds, she turns away from us and faces the wall.

"Grandma," says Takashi, who used to sit beside her along the river, as a boy, talking about the light on the water, "we've come all this way to see you!" He steps to the head of the bed, to address the back of her neck. "Everyone's here. Don't you want to see your great-granddaughter?"

No sound emerges from the body in the bed.

"We're worried, Grandma," he goes on, always kindly and protective. "We don't want you to be sick."

It takes determination, I'm sure, but the old woman doesn't stir.

"Grandma," says Takashi's nine-year-old cousin, a soft boy

with shiny hair and a sweet manner, who now steps forwards to address her back. "Won't you play cards with us? I've been waiting!"

Nothing. If all of you are going to close your doors on me, she might be thinking, why should I have any time for you? A husband gone, a son missing, a daughter who's placed her in a nursing home: it isn't hard to understand why she's gone on strike.

Concerned glances flash among the small group gathered around the bed. The nurses and doctors have so many people to deal with who are suffering from nothing but old age that they are always busy.

Finally, Hiroko steps up. I've seen how the season's complications have drained her of some of her brightness and left her confused and pale at times, but she's never been slow to seize an occasion by its throat.

"Grandma," she says—she might be talking again to her kids when they were young—"what's up? We've all come to see you; we love you. Why do you want to make us sad?"

The body in the bed might be gone already; it doesn't stir.

"You want to make us all suffer? You want your daughter to be an orphan? Already this year, I've lost Grandpa. Now . . ." A nurse comes in and hurries away, looking terrified as Hiroko's voice rises. "Now you want to take Grandmother away from me, too?"

The body squirms deeper under the sheets, as if to place itself outside the reach of words.

"You always say I'm selfish," Hiroko goes on. "But what about this? Why do you want us all to be miserable? Think of how we'll feel if you're gone, too."

Then, coming up with an unexpected flourish: "You don't want to see your son? What if Masahiro comes? He's been missing you for so long. What if he comes to visit and you're not here?"

The figure remains motionless, and Hiroko turns around and says, "Let's go."

The next day, however, when the two of us return, a nurse greets us at the elevator. The old woman didn't want a soul to notice, the nurse whispers, but she could be seen nibbling a little in the night. There's every sign that something in her has turned.

We walk to the bed, and my aged mother-in-law, catching sight of Hiroko, clamps her hands to her ears to block her daughter out.

"Okay, Grandma, if you want to deprive us of everything, to deprive yourself, if you want to keep this up . . ."

As we go back out into the street—"Strike over!" Hiroko announces—the sun is blazing, and we gird ourselves for the next typhoon.

Now, weeks later, everywhere I go, I see Masahiro: the fact that I've never seen him in real life means he inhabits every face. That could be him outside the Kerala restaurant, I think;

I know he teaches at the culture center across the street. That smallish man at the Dostoevsky shelf at the bookstore: might he not be the one who told Hiroko when they were young that blue skies are for kids?

I've seen him in photographs, but the photographs come from half a century ago. Still, I can recognize the bright confidence, the way his peaked cap is tilted above his Prussian school uniform, the determined eyebrows: his father's son at every turn. Hiroko routinely refers to him as a turtle—he always called her a hare—and yet she never forgets that he always pointed out that the turtle won the race in the end. Retracting his head does not have to mean he's ready to recede into the background.

"I small time," Hiroko told me recently—though she's told me before, as the dusty memories become most of what she has—"always my brother little protect me. One day, so rainy day, he say, 'Little sister, I carry your book.' Even he cannot carry his own book!

"So rainy day, he has umbrella"—she delivers a typically spot-on rendition of a small boy struggling with an umbrella and a pile of books, even as he's weighed down by a full satchel—"but he say, he must do this. Always so big protector."

"But you told me he was always sick."

"Yes." She nods gravely. "Not so strong."

Whenever her father tried to throw her into the closet, she says—I can see the scene unfold—she clung to the knob so fiercely that he had to admit defeat. But her brother regularly lost that same struggle. As they ate, she and her parents could hear him shouting, "Please, let me out! Please! It's so dark in here. I'm scared."

Hiroko would always be an outdoors person, exploring the garden, or wandering into neighbors' backyards to collect crabs for schoolyard crustacean-fights, while her brother was sequestered in his room with his books. But she never denies his fortitude and determination. "My brother not so usual Japanese," she tells me now. "Me, my father, also not so usual, but he so different."

In elementary school, she says, he declared he wouldn't learn the abacus because he was sure more sophisticated computational machines would be coming soon; upon graduation, as his father urged him towards a business course, he announced he was going to study psychology. After its loss in war, he knew that Japan would face no end of problems of the soul.

Upon my arrival in Japan, I'd read that there were all of four registered psychologists in the whole of Tokyo, population eight million. Traditional societies turn to grandmothers— to temples or the community—for their solace. But, like his sister, like his father, Masahiro was never going to fit into a society in which to be as bland and invisible as a grain of rice, at least on the surface, was the price of admission.

When I invited Hiroko's father on his only foreign holiday, to California, he installed himself at the counter at Sushiya on Sunset Boulevard (as at every such Japanese restaurant up and down the coast) and told the bewildered chef preparing *uni*, "My son studied in Kansas: the only boy in the neighborhood to go abroad! He got his doctoral degree at the Jung Institute, in Zürich, the fourth Japanese ever to do so. Writing his dissertation in English, but living in German!"

When we took my father-in-law on drives, he spoke so much about his missing son—pride giving way to anger before winning out again—that Hiroko had to remind him that he had another child, and she was right there, by his side.

I don't need to reflect that, were I to run into my brother-in-law—and if we had no relation—I'd probably have more to share with him than with any of my neighbors. As a boy, Hiroko tells me, he devoured Goethe, Nietzsche, Tolstoy; she turned to Hesse only because that was the one foreign author of the time her brother hadn't claimed (blue skies and a sense of possibility were for kids). And yet, if he began to guess who I was in relation to him, his other side might flare out.

When Hiroko introduced him to her best friend, she tells me, he greeted the not-so-confident woman with "You really think you're beautiful?" And when a friend of his confessed that he liked Masahiro's sister, Masahiro said to him, "My sister thinks you look like an animal!" They never saw the friend smile again. Following his own complicated logic, Hiroko's brother announced that he was cutting off the family because Hiroko was getting a divorce.

"Maybe he was worried that he'd have to support you if you ended up alone with your kids," I say. "And then support your parents, too, if you couldn't look after them."

"Maybe." She shrugs, genuinely perplexed. "I don't know."

Then, continuing: "I have only one speed. Always fastball. But my brother not so straight. Only curveball. Change-up. Slider." One of her graces is to radiate transparency; her brother is the question mark in the corner of every room.

To enter Japan through the narrow gateway of ping-pong: it didn't sound like any of the loftier ideas I'd had when I came over to Kyoto, weighed down with readings of old poets and philosophers. I'd moved to Japan, I thought, to learn how to live with less hurry and fear of time, and to see how an old and seasoned culture makes its peace with the passing hours. I'd moved there to learn how best to dissolve a sense of self within something larger and less temporary.

But now to step into the health club—or, on Saturdays, the old, drafty gym—feels like stepping into the thick of a society in the middle of a convivial, long-running drama in which I have to tease out every turn and nuance.

One local friend, impossibly slim, poker-faced, as speedy as someone sorting letters into piles, is switching her paddle from left hand to right in the middle of a point, to flip the ball devastatingly into the opposite court. A cheerful neighbor twists his wrist around and hits a gawky penholder backhand spinning fast across the net. The tall woman who sports a frilly black skirt above her leggings and tells us how she came here from Korea thirty-five years ago curtsies between points, even as she's standing almost as far back as the mirrored wall, hitting textbook chops.

For so much of the day, our neighbors are standing in front of these mirrors, practicing how to become Margot Fonteyn, how to die like a Russian swan; for me, the studio is my classroom for learning how to play at being Japanese. How to be invisible, and how to read the unwritten rules that guide us; how to compete not to win but to make sure that as many people as possible can feel that they are winners. How, in short, to be a voice within a choral symphony, and not a soloist tootling off on his own.

Soon after Hiroko quietly urged me to give the game a try, nine years ago—I'd played as a boy, she remembered, and now our local health club was rolling out some tables—I stepped into the studio, to be greeted by a smooth, warm man in his late sixties, with rimless glasses and some words of English. Next to him was a smiling, shiningly gracious woman who might have been welcoming me to an elegant dinner party.

As they introduced me round—"Pico-san's a writer! He comes from California"—the "Emperor," as I began to think of him, inducted me into the customs of the place: the sign-up sheet, the thirty-minute segments, the way we had to run up and down the studio in parallel lines with mops as soon as we were through, to make sure that the space was as immaculate as when we entered. Then he started seeking out players of my level with whom I could practice.

Very soon, however, I sensed that it was everything silent, as always in Japan, that bound us together. My friends were exceptional when practicing; even the weakest players could keep a high-speed rally going for minutes. But get them into a game and hit it where they weren't expecting it and they were instantly at a loss. They were born for duets, I realized; playing with each other was their strength, treating each other as a part of themselves, as in a dance or an act of love. Playing against each other never would be.

I learned, therefore, never to say a word about the result of any game, even though some of the women (most notably Mayumi-san) would hoot and improvise a war dance if they scored a victory. In any case, we switched off pairs so rapidly that nobody lost for long—and two-set games guaranteed there weren't so many losers. If ever there was just one person in the room when I arrived, I learned never to contemplate a game of singles; our job was to rally with each other until two others showed up and practiced enough to be ready for some doubles.

I learned not to leave so long as there were even numbers in the studio—one person's departure would throw three others out—and how, discreetly, to leave as soon as a newcomer arrived, if that left us with an odd number. And if I did go home before the others, I had to turn towards everyone when I reached the door, bow deeply and say, "Please excuse me for leaving before the rest of you."

One afternoon, as I was exchanging forehands with the Federer-graceful Empress, her husband placed a kindly hand on my shoulder and said, "Pico-san, why don't you hit a few with Nakai-san?" Nakai-san was a tiny man, with a sweet, clumsy smile and the air of a geek, not least because he was the only one to come into the studio carrying a stylish man-purse instead of an Adidas bag full of equipment. He hit my balls back, but always a little tentatively, like a boy in a science lab who's trying to pour some semi-poisonous liquid into a test tube. I learned how to take spin off my shots so he could always block them back, and soon we were something of a dance team ourselves.

One bright morning, I saw him stepping out of a long, very new black Mercedes outside the post office, leaving the engine running, and realized, many months too late: Nakai-san was a professional gangster, the rare soul who had decided to ignore that section of the health-club registration form that requests every prospective member to confirm, "I have no tattoos," and "I am not a member of any criminal organization." And I was the ideal person to be encouraged to play with him, as a kind of outlier, too.

I thought back to the gym, where flirty, ultra-feminine Ms. Teraki, the septuagenarian with the sweeping masculine strokes, sought me out each week. The same principle, I realized: she must be a member of the parallel universe that is the night world—the proprietress of a bar, perhaps—so the others almost imperceptibly left the foreigner to take her on. Everyone was cordial to her, full of laughs and warmth, but when we paired off, she was the one routinely left behind.

My friends always made allowances for me when I didn't put my name on the sign-up sheet, or inscribed it in roman letters in the box for hula dancing by mistake; only one man whispered behind his paddle to his wife, "You see! He never signs up, and still they let him play!" The women, after almost every shot, cried, "Amazing!" or "Pico-san's balls are so incredible," even though many Japanese men in our circle were far more skilled. When Hiroko came to meet me at the studio once, she marveled, "You've become a teen idol!" She never guessed that her bedraggled, hairless husband would become a kind of mascot, a sporty proto-Bieber in his mid-fifties.

My role, I saw, was to develop a kind of social penholder grip, to match the one so many of my friends deployed with their paddles: to pass as a local, just another member of the community, whenever possible, though to be able to flip over to be the token foreigner whenever that would enhance the happiness and harmony of the whole.

The equinox is not many days behind us, but already we can feel a pinch in the air, a draft of something chill. It will go and come back again over the refulgent days of October, but it's like a premonition of sorts, the first knock on the door from a visitor who will pull us closer and closer to the cold and dark. I find myself watching now for the days when Hiroko complains of a crick in her neck, or starts to cough; her twinges become mine.

"You remember when your father died?" Hiroko says, coming out onto our tiny terrace, where there's barely room for the washing machine and me on my kid's blue folding chair, the laundry flapping in my face. She shivers; sunshine and warmth are taking their leave of each other as the season turns.

It's hard to forget the rainy-season day on which the phone began to rattle in the dark, and I heard a half-familiar voice telling me my father had been rushed to the hospital back in

California. Pneumonia, I was told; the small, noxious brown Madison cigarillos he'd been smoking for twenty years had knocked the strength out of his lungs.

I flew back that day, and for two weeks, my mother and I watched him, eyes closed, in his bed, the numbers on the monitor going up and down. We descended into the sunny courtyard to take lunch, my mother trying to will him back into the world even as I wondered if, perhaps, at sixty-five, he'd had enough; not so much to look forward to, other than regrets.

Then, just after Father's Day, one day before the longest day of the year, we arrived in another bright, silent dawn to see that the ups and downs were over and the line on the monitor was as flat and changeless as he was.

"I never met your father," Hiroko says, and it's true; I'd worried that he might blame his son's defection from the world of financial security and achievement on her.

But then I catch myself, and remember: the books scattered across my desk, the nonsense songs with which I was serenading her ten minutes ago, the occasional fluency that even I don't trust.

"Don't worry," I say. "You're keeping him company every day."

The lemon scent of *kinmokusei*—daphne, as I'd taken the local flower to be—is perfuming the lanes now. Hiroko draws me closer to a bush in the park, so I can catch the full air-freshener impact. There are plastic leaves fluttering off the lampposts of central Nara, and signs for "Maple Lattes" and "Chestnut Sundays" along the busy streets. In our local supermarket, someone has drawn a picture of a maple leaf, and the matrons have long since prepared moon-shaped rice balls to eat on the day of the harvest moon. The season's beginning to pick up momentum as heat softens in the days.

Hiroko, though, seems at times to have cast off in a little boat across a wide lake thick with mist. In all the years I've known her, I've never sensed a gap, something important that she can't get across to me, or I to her. But now there's something remote in her at times, beyond even the probate work she has to do, the forms to complete, the many ways in Japan she has to work to take care of her father in the afterworld. As we walk through the deer park, she still breaks into the deep voice of a stag, saying, "Hello, Pico, where have you been?" She chatters merrily about the friends of mine she refers to as "Miss Rabbit" and "Bison" and "Million Yen Mark." But sometimes I can hardly recognize the small, accelerating figure who was roaring around the neighborhood on her Honda Hurricane not so long ago, I the bulging-eyed passenger clinging to her back.

"So strange," she says today, and then stands absolutely motionless in a wash of light. "Almost I can feel my father inside me. I not Hiroko."

"That's good, isn't it?"

"Good, but so strange. Almost I not here."

Then, without warning, as she moves towards the refrigerator, her face crumbles and she collapses into racking sobs, this invincible spirit who handled everything with such aplomb in remaking her and her mother's lives overnight. I stand up and hold her, and she lets out all that's been gathering inside for weeks, the rending gasps starting up again each time they begin to subside.

Then, almost visibly collecting herself, she says, "I'm sorry," and heads towards her dresser to prepare for the world.

That evening, returning from Kyoto, she says, "Sachi so thin now. So elegant." She turns on her phone to show me pictures of our daughter, in a shapely indigo dress, looking like a magazine cover with her bright smile and ponytail, though her oversized dark glasses reveal her to be very much her mother's girl.

"It's just the uncertainty," I say. "The waiting."

I try to banish the images of women wasting away for love that I've met in nineteenth-century novels. I try to assure Hiroko that our daughter could not be in better health physically.

Four years after we moved into this area—good schools, safe streets, forty-five seconds on foot from our flat to post office and bus stop and supermarket and clinic, with a seven-hundred-dollar monthly rent that never seems to increase—Sachi, then thirteen, started to lose weight. She'd always been blessed with the big-boned, red-cheeked health of her father, and she excelled at the backstroke in the swimming pool, the forehand on the tennis court; she and her brother had uncomplainingly adapted to wearing headphones when they wanted to watch TV because a strange foreigner called Pico was sleeping on the living-room couch, and to inhabiting a space so cramped that we could not open our bathroom door by more than seventeen inches.

But now—was it puberty?—she was growing leaner and more delicate by the season, ever more irresistible to her brother's high-school friends, willowy and long-legged.

A doctor assured us she was fine—girls change at this age—but six months later, we felt we had to consult him again. He told us everything was as it should be, and then he said, "Oh, wait a minute . . ." and went into the next room, where his textbooks were. When he returned, he looked like a man on the run. "I'm sorry," he said, "but your daughter has Hodgkin's disease. It's almost unknown in Japan. That's why I didn't catch it before. It's now in Stage Three; you must get her into a hospital tomorrow."

Sachi cried for a few minutes, and then she picked up her culture's sense that an argument with reality is one you'll never win, and never cried again. Together with her mother, she gathered her sketchpad and her pens, a Jewel CD and a few textbooks, and took the three trains to Kyoto; three weeks before her fourteenth birthday, she was just young enough to qualify for the pediatric oncology ward. Soccer stars came by to rally spirits, young nurses allowed her to prop a small black-and-white TV on her table. Next to almost every bed, in the Japanese fashion, was a mother, who slept in a chair by her child, for a year or as long as it took.

But over the twelve months she was in the ward, Sachi saw

the beds around her slowly empty out. The mothers, with smiles, made their apologies and went back home. Most of the patients, seven- or eight-year-olds with leukemia, were never to be seen again.

Meanwhile, all kinds of other surprises began to rain down on us, as if to bring home how every blessing, like every curse, comes from nowhere, unmerited. We would not have to pay a penny, the doctors at Kyoto University Hospital informed us one evening; Hodgkin's was so rare in Japan that students and researchers were grateful to have a chance to observe it up close on a real-life patient. And then, equally out of the blue, a letter from a nearby university announced—though no one there knew of her current predicament—that Sachi would not have to go through Japan's infamous "examination hell" to gain admission to its hallways, so long as she agreed to bring her enthusiasm for learning English into a major in Spanish.

Her brother and I, back in the apartment, took to bonding over delivery pizza and nightly broadcasts of Hanshin Tigers baseball games; Hiroko, most evenings, once her job was finished, took a sixty-minute ride through the dark to the hospital, to sleep by her daughter's side. When Sachi emerged, one autumn later, she was closer to her mother than ever and seemed wiser than her classmates, and not only because of the teacher who came to her bed to make sure she didn't miss out on her lessons. But even that happy ending—sixteen years have shown no signs of recurrence—leaves an echo.

We look now at the picture of our daughter, and don't know whether to shiver or rejoice.

. . .

With the first of October—the day when, traditionally, the Japanese begin preparing themselves for winter—Hiroko erupts into a kind of "baby spring" cleaning that's no spectacle for the faint of heart; it reminds me of the typhoon that swept through last week, sending cars around the neighborhood all night long to broadcast warnings, while our TV screen filled with stranded passengers at airports and departure boards that read "Canceled." I'm still in bed as I sense her running—literally—through our two rooms, picking up every stray piece of lint or paper she can find. She's rushing through the junk mail that's assembled near the telephone and sweeping items into a ball, gathering up the pair of jeans I set out to wear today, and adding it to an ungainly pile to fling into the washing machine on the terrace.

Our family history is a litany of the treasures she's been far too eager to clean. The armband Takashi got autographed by his favorite heavy-metal guitarist that she mistakenly hurled into the machine. My green shirt with the tag "Wash by Hand" that came out from the washing machine a perfect size for one of the Seven Dwarves. The cute fox her daughter's teacher gave the little girl upon graduation from second grade, whose stomach looked even grimier than before it went through a spin cycle.

I can hear keys still jangling in my trouser pockets as they revolve in the gurgling machine. But by now Hiroko is sweeping everything she can find into two large garbage bags, for me to take out to the designated street corner three days from now, then slip-sliding across the wooden floor with a cloth under her foot before pulling out a vacuum cleaner to poke into the area where my notes are stacked, leaving me worried that now 2006 is above 2011, with 2003 in the next prefecture.

It's her compulsion, I realize, the way she gets her energy out. "She's a beautiful storm," marvels a young friend who's visiting from California. "It's like you get picked up in this fast breeze and carried somewhere you can't guess at. You don't know what's going on, but it all feels magical, a kind of dream."

"Don't worry," I assure him. "She has no idea where she's going, either." It's one of the qualities I most admire in her: she doesn't stop to think. She's so caught up in this moment that she seldom looks back, to her first marriage or the many things she's left behind; apart from worrying about her daughter, she doesn't bother much with needless thoughts about the future. "I'm sorry, I little crazy lady," she brightly announced to this friend when they first met. "My son say I have only accelerator. No brake!" And though every decision she makes is crazy, it always proves the right one.

Every autumn, when I return to our apartment after visiting my mother, it's to find the whole place rearranged: in an overflow of energy, Hiroko has moved the piano—a substantial piece of furniture in so tiny a place—and in the process transformed both rooms. The Van Morrison CDs I'd tried to protect from the domestic hurricane are now stashed in some pretty, frilly box where I'll never see them again; the magazines I spent long afternoons sorting into piles last autumn have been mixed up higgledy-piggledy again, and stashed into a black shopping bag on whose cover is written, unfathomably, "Global Collective Unconscious Mind! See on earth now it in heaven."

Sometimes this radical freedom from care, as if my wife were herself as implacable as autumn winds, can make for problems in quiet, ever-cautious Japan; but a part of me can't help admiring her fluency in the realm of action. Out—as I try to avert my eyes at my desk—come the long black boots from the closet, the gloves and sweaters that she's stashed in closets through the spring and summer; out come cashmere scarves and heavy socks. Sandals and thin blouses get put away for hibernation; my shapeless black down jacket emerges from its hiding place, and I gratefully stuff its four capacious pockets with granola bars and Proust.

Whenever the day is cloudless like this, Hiroko pulls open all the windows and screen doors, and hauls the futons out to our tiny terrace to catch the sun; she carries out carpets and towels and every last item from toilet and bathroom so they can bask in fresh air and come back renewed. That's who she is, of course: dust never settles on her for long. She's so unlined and bright-eyed that strangers often mistake her either for my daughter or, less happily, for some young beauty whose company I'm renting in old age. In California, I get asked if I want a senior discount while she, ten months older, gets carded if she orders a beer.

Today, she flings herself down in an exhausted heap after the torrential burst of cleaning, pale and completely spent. An hour later, she leaps out of bed and starts buttoning herself into a long black dress and short boots, turquoise scarf knotted around her neck.

"We little go shrine?"

I know better than to remind her that going to the shrine was the habit of her mother's she most complained about when we first met. As vexing as her mother's way of calling up every day to complain about her husband—or shouting out prayers in a freezing shower every morning, to appease the Shinto gods.

"*Tsuku-tsuku-boshi*," she tells me brightly now, as we walk across the park. "Little sound of summer ending. Not bird; cricket. Special sound of cricket when summer ends."

Then we catch a whirring in the air beside us, a red dragonfly. "*Aka tombo*," she explains. "This means autumn coming soon. Little autumn messenger insect."

I might be walking through a beginner's guide to the season, with the covers thrown wide open. I know many more of our neighbors than she does, spending all day at home, and joining in the communal rounds of ping-pong and watching the maple leaves rising to a blaze in the park; but she knows the flowers and the winds that create a frame for the human pantomime.

As we descend the flight of hidden steps, she goes on, "Little old person house," pointing to a large wooden structure. "Day-care service, but for very old kids. This is where they train police dogs." She's gesturing towards a wide driveway and palatial house.

"It looks silent. Maybe there aren't so many customers?"

"Many," she upbraids me. "These dogs are learning to be silent."

She points out an early persimmon tree in front of a two-story villa. "This one you cannot eat. We call *shibugaki*, keep in house, one, two week. Little dry fruit feeling." Then, a few feet later, *"Yuzu."* Citrusy flavors of Japan are everywhere in the autumn.

"Sometimes," Hiroko goes on—the rice paddies are exquisitely tended on one side of us—"my grandpa see thief running, with vegetable. He little 'Pfft!'" She makes a sound like wind escaping through a door. "Thief stop. He cannot move!"

Her late father was the one famous for his ghost stories; neighborhood kids gathered at his feet to feel the chills stealing down their spine. The only other time he found a group around him was when, in old age, he started going to the elders' day-care center; we opened up its monthly newsletter to see a picture of him drawing, amidst a circle of other gray-hairs. He'd never had much in the way of friends before.

As we near the shrine, Hiroko peels off and stands by the side.

"What is it?"

"I cannot go."

"But you came all this way!"

She looks at me, not for the first time, as if I don't understand a thing. "I cannot shrine this year." For one year after a death in the family, a person is polluted, and must not bring her scent of death into the place of gods. She cannot send out New Year's cards this year, and if she lived closer to tradition, she'd be wearing black every day for twelve months.

I pass alone under the torii gate, make my ablutions, and rehearse my jet-lagged routine of early autumn.

Back in the apartment, Hiroko starts wrestling the futons into the room again—she wants no help from a malfunctioning husband, who will only make things worse—and bustles around, hair now swept into an elegant ponytail, beating the dirt from the carpets and taking the table mats out from the sun.

"Summer little ending," she says, settling down at last. "Now come autumn."

Sometimes Hiroko's cousin sees Masahiro walking down the street outside his analyst's office in southern Kyoto, not many minutes from where his mother now lives. "He just walks past me, as if he hasn't seen." Sometimes, Hiroko says, she sees him in the same place.

"Really? Are you sure?"

"Of course! I know my brother! One time, I little call to him, 'Older brother, older brother!' But never he turn round."

"Maybe, with your cousin, he didn't recognize her. It's been a long time."

"Doesn't want recognize. They always so close. Too close! More close than me."

"It's the same in my mother's family," I remind her. "The same in my father's. One brother cutting off everyone, usually over property. All families are the same."

"I worry about my son," she says. "Sometimes I looking him, I see my brother." She stops. "But he cut me, it's okay. I not always so kind before. He cannot forget."

Even on our honeymoon, fourteen years ago, when I took Hiroko to meet the Dalai Lama in his home in Dharamsala— "Prepare one question," I'd told her, "something that matters the most to you"—she'd asked about her brother.

"Maybe you should write to him," the Tibetan monk said, turning to me with his doctor's no-nonsense pragmatism.

"Because I'm not part of the family?"

"Also"—he laughed heartily—"not Japanese!"

So I did, though, like all Hiroko's regular greetings to Masahiro, it disappeared into an unanswering blank space.

This year, however, for the first time in almost a quarter of a century, she exchanged words with him.

Her father had left no will when he died, and although everyone knew what it would have said—a third to his wife, a third to his daughter, a third to the long-lost prodigal whose achievements made him glow—that didn't help with the law. Or with a son who, fifteen minutes away, declined to exchange a word.

Hiroko managed to find a friend of a cousin's daughter's school friend who dealt with probate and estate questions, and asked him if he'd help. The three of us gathered on the tatami mat in the room in her parents' house presided over by the small, framed photo of her ashen father and her long-dead grandmother. Our young visitor, in his ill-fitting suit, shifted uncomfortably—we might have been sitting inside a grave— while assuring us it was no problem.

"I know these cases," he said. "It's my job to deal with them."

He went off with Masahiro's particulars, simply to get formal verification from the missing son that the dead father's property could be dispersed as logic suggested.

A few days later, the lawyer got back to us. "I'm sorry," he said, "I've never encountered a case like this. I called and called the number you gave me; he never answered. So I went to his apartment. I could hear someone inside; I could hear the TV. But I rang and rang and no one answered."

I suppose they'd seen a stranger's face through the peephole, and reacted as Hiroko does when she sees a Jehovah's Witness or someone from public television requesting a monthly donation.

"I've run out of options; I slipped something under the door, and someone slipped it right back at me."

"I'll try," said Hiroko.

Scanning online, Sachi found that her elusive uncle taught a class in central Kyoto on Tuesdays at 6:00 p.m., explaining the psychology of Jung. Weeks of preparing herself later, Hiroko decided to ambush her brother there, and Sachi gamely offered to come along as an emotional bodyguard.

They arrived at 5:00 p.m. and waited while a few members of the class drifted in.

"You're interested in Jung?" an old woman asked Hiroko.

"No. I'm just here to meet your teacher. What's he like?"

"So cool," said the woman. "We're all in love with him."

"I'll say!" said another student. "Such a good teacher. Like a movie star."

Then Hiroko heard the elevator doors open and saw Masahiro emerge. Though he had not officially laid eyes on her in years, he registered her presence instantly, and beckoned her to a corner.

"Look," he said, determined that it be just the two of them, "we'll talk over there." And then: "I have just two things to say to you. All the letters, the postcards you've sent, every one for twenty years, I've read them. Every one. And the second thing I have to say is this: I've cut off the family forever. I never want to have anything to do with anyone."

He looked cool, Hiroko told me, in a European cap; he hadn't lost their father's sense of style. Who knew but he was still a fervent supporter of the Hiroshima Carp, the hometown baseball team their father had taught his children to support?

She told him about the paper he had to sign, and he said that if she sent it to him he would sign it (and he did).

Then, with Sachi beside her, Hiroko went down in the elevator to take the train home. "She couldn't stop crying," Sachi told me, of her famously fearless mother, whose emotions, in so many colors, were jouncing around in a kind of washing machine after she met the sibling she so missed and loved.

Even now, telling me the story, Hiroko chokes over her words, and I can barely hear her as she speaks.

It was on an October day as warm as this that I was formally introduced to Hiroko's parents, twenty-three years ago. They didn't know exactly who I was in their daughter's and grand-children's lives, but it wouldn't have taken much to surmise: Hiroko was in a closet-sized apartment near the celebrated castle of southern Kyoto, the trains rumbling past even here, and she was ceremonially introducing them to someone she seemed to have known for quite a while.

Her father—a bantam eagerness, a shy, strong-toothed grin, a careful courtesy that, in my case, translated into instant, undiscriminating friendliness—gave me a firm handshake, sat down and, coming from a world in which men are unchallenged bosses, began to speak.

"In Siberia, during the war, there were wolves everywhere, and when the wolves began eating us"—or was it that the men were eating the wolves?—"we thought we'd left the mortal world behind. We knew that many of us were fated to die! And when the Russians came to inspect us a little later . . ."

Hiroko and her mother looked away and went about their business—her mother was used to tuning her husband out, and Hiroko would often tell me that her father's stories were a "stuck record." I, meanwhile, abandoned by the two women, made desperate efforts to discern where the pauses in the story came, and said, "Isn't that the truth?" whenever I sensed one, or "You really don't say!"

Never had my future father-in-law enjoyed such a respon-sive audience. "All our commanders had run away! Or died. So we were lost, lost in the wilderness. And then the Russians found us. But if they hadn't . . ."

I looked over to see what the other two were doing, and I noticed that Hiroko's mother was sobbing and sobbing, as at a funeral. Her face was down-turned and she was not making much noise, but her shoulders were rising and falling, rising and falling, as if her heart were slowly coming apart.

It could have been the sound of her husband's war stories, but I got very much the feeling that it was simply the sight of me.

"Come on, Grandma," said Hiroko. "Don't do that!"

"I'm sorry," gasped the old woman, then in her early sixties. She threw a typically charming and welcoming smile at me. "My daughter's crazy, isn't she? The two of them. They never stop fighting."

"Grandma!"

"And then the Russians said, 'Any soldier who wants to can leave. . . .'"

The old woman was still weeping. Just what I always feared, she might have been thinking, looking at the stranger with Indian features across the table; even when she was young, my daughter was too interested in Taj Mahal and elephants.

Hiroko spent much of the evening loudly berating her mother, and the tiny old woman with the wrinkled, tanned face and the short gray hair didn't try to fight back, but only adopted a beleaguered attitude that suggested that life had made an arranged marriage for her, with misery.

Meanwhile, Hiroko's father was continuing unabated. "And then I went up to the commander of the prisoner-of-war camp and said, 'It's not fair to give us so little to eat! We'll starve.' 'I like your honesty,' the man said, and after that, we never lacked for food, and . . ."

Years later, I'd see that the evening was not so distant from the ping-pong practice in which two entirely different pairs kept hitting balls at the same time, across the diagonal; Hiroko's father would always throw his arms around any stranger, however criminal, while his wife would despair at any prospective son-in-law, whoever he might be.

"And at the end of the war"—these details would get filled in for me later by Hiroko—"I was free to leave. In 1948. So I wrote to my mother in Hiroshima to say I was coming home. But in the chaos of the time, my letter never arrived. So I went back to Hiroshima—there was nothing there, my hometown was just rubble—and I was walking down the main street when I happened to pass my mother.

"'Mother!' I shouted.

"'What?' she cried. 'Do you have feet?'

"She assumed I was a ghost! She thought she was hallucinating the ghost of her son who'd died at war. She'd never received my letter, and she couldn't believe it was me, her long-lost son, walking past her down the street."

In Japan, Hiroko reminded me, ghosts don't have feet.

Her mother, all the while, continued sobbing silently into her cup of green tea, inconsolable. She would always be cordial to me—her eyes full of merriment and puckishness—but her outburst was a quiet reminder that she would feel so much happier if I were just six thousand miles away.

Hiroko and her mother never stopped bickering all evening long—"No, Grandma! That's not true!" "Why do you always do this to me?" As we dispersed, however, close to midnight,

Hiroko threw her arms around the older lady and they walked arm in arm down the street, like the closest, most loving friends in the world, all warmth and affection.

Hiroko's father continued beaming at me, overwhelmed that he had found someone so enraptured by his tales of Manchuria and the sudden song he broke into, about his friends lying in the ground, and the sun beginning to set as he dreamed of his hometown far away. Before long, he was referring to me as his best friend in the world.

At the time, I'd been surprised that, contrary to my experience so far, it was a Japanese man who was instantly warm and a woman who kept her distance. Now, looking back, I'm touched by how eagerly my future father-in-law was trying to make contact with the wider world in any form; his loneliness and his longing for adventure would always be of a piece. All this proud son of Hiroshima wanted, I'd come to see, was to enjoy the freedom of America.

"Pi-sama, welcome home!"

Sachi, our sparklingly bright-eyed, openhearted daughter is waving to me and jumps up from her chair to give me an un-Japanese hug as I arrive in the Starbucks outlet that occupies perhaps the choicest location in Kyoto: next to Sanjo Bridge, where fifty-two Christians were once publicly burned to death, children clinging to their mothers' backs while others sang the "Te Deum." Today, as if to stretch summer out by a few weeks, it still has a wooden deck open for looking out on the Kamo River and on the eastern hills a few long blocks away. Like many a resourceful Japanese girl, Sachi fled Japan as soon as she could, moving to Spain and a Spanish boyfriend almost the day she graduated from university here; she's been living in Spain (and Spanish) for eight years. But she'd come back after her grandfather's death, and stayed around to help her mother with paperwork and visits to the nursing home.

"You're ready?" I say, because it's another "second summer" morning—bright days in October become a regular miracle, the more glorious because they still seem unexpected—and it's hard to stay indoors when the unearned brilliance is so dazzling. All Kyoto seems out today. As we walk towards the hills, Sachi fills me in happily on friends from high school, their husbands, the drawings she's selling online, not least of the fox shrine near her grandparents' house, and all the whimsical ghosts and spirits she's superimposing upon the photographs she's taken. That mention of "husbands" is a slippery one, though I'm less anxious than her mother might be. Sachi's brother, like most Japanese males, followed a more conventional course—going to Tokyo as soon as he graduated, getting a job with a good, solid company (Japan Airlines), finding a sweetheart at twenty-five, settling down with his wife, his little girl and his steady, if not always exhilarating work. But Japanese women still have no good place in the system, so either they defect—as Hiroko had done by marrying me—or they try to make the most of the free time that being denied most public opportunity can bring.

In Sachi's case, she'd brought her beau home to us, and her

mother and I had both been charmed and relieved to meet such an engaging, funny, quick-witted, handsome guy. "Francisco," as I'll call him, could go shopping with Hiroko—I'd never met a young male who so loved clothes—and could talk Scorsese and Oliver Stone with me, when he wasn't cracking both of us up with renditions of a clumsy swimmer at the Olympics. As we walked through the narrow lanes of Kyoto's geisha quarter, he told us how fetching he'd look in a kimono and wooden shoes. It wasn't hard to see how innocent, accommodating Sachi had been wowed by someone who seemed as bright and colorful as her mother.

But as we got to see him more, both Hiroko and I began to wonder why he was changing his clothes four times a day and applying makeup before he slept. I'm not used to meeting Spanish males who travel long distances to hear George Michael in concert—who yearn in fact to consult George Michael for life decisions—and who continue to worship Michael Jackson long after his death. Francisco started to sprout male friends round every corner—Misha and Juan and Daisuke—and I began to wonder if, in his early thirties, he'd come to discover who he really was, and found it to be someone different from the one who'd fallen in love with a sweet and trusting Japanese girl he'd met at twenty-four.

He'd accompanied Sachi back to Japan in the difficult days after her grandfather's death, as if he had all the time in the world (we never could quite tell what he did for a living). He was always kind, strikingly good at finding his place within a complicated Japanese family, able to charm everyone he met. But after he'd flown back to Spain, he told Sachi to hang on.

Days passed, and then weeks; soon months were speeding by. She waited by the phone, and I began to realize she was patient enough to wait forever. Francisco surely knew that, too; he came to China—less than three hours away by plane—and never flew over to visit her. He didn't invite her to come and see him, either. She waited and waited, growing slimmer and more glamorous by the week, till she was wearing dresses many sizes smaller than before. He'd come to Japan soon, he said, and I began to see how "soon" in his language meant "tomorrow," and *"mañana"* could easily mean "never."

Now I take pains not quite to broach the subject as I walk with my newly model-thin, determinedly cheerful young daughter through the autumn sunshine. She's inherited Hiroko's rare mix of beauty and innocence—she doesn't notice the men who steal glances at her—but where Hiroko can never stop moving, Sachi, by her own admission, can barely start. She's still more Japanese than her restless and rebellious mother, and where Hiroko whizzes around in a kind of spin cycle of her own, gentle Sachi is a picture book of sweet normalcy.

"It must be quiet in your big house," I say; Sachi's in the two-story home owned by her grandparents, a three-minute walk down a canal from the wooden house near the fox shrine. The same house, in fact, that her runaway uncle and his family occupied after they came back from the Jung Institute in Switzerland.

"Oh no," she sings back. "I have lots of friends."

"And Francisco?"

"He's busy. He said to say hello. We Skyped last night."

What better than to have a sweet, helpful friend on hold for whenever he needs something in Japan? The men who walk past us shoot looks at us, hazarding guesses as to why a wintry bum is accompanied by a picture of spring.

"He didn't say anything about coming over?"

"He's really busy right now," she says, and even the timbre of her bright response, just one tone quieter than usual, tells me to ask no more.

"Shall we go all the way to Kiyomizu?" I say. The Temple of Pure Water towers over the whole city, via a squiggle of picturesque streets and elegant slopes.

"Of course! I'm so happy to take a walk with you," says Sachi, who never complains, and even in the hospital, in great pain, went out of her way not to betray sadness or anger.

We walk through the brightness of the golden day, and I try to fight off the thought that our daughter's looking as beautiful and thin as when she was thirteen, reduced by sickness.

And all the while, the games of ping-pong go on, the way a river might sparkle past even as fires begin to rise above it in the parks. At first the players are a blur to me, other than the poised Emperor and Empress who preside over everything. The women mostly have jet-black hair above their pink T-shirts and dark slacks, though it doesn't always go with their eyebrows; in the health club, they wear pink locker-keys around their wrists as surely as the men wear blue. A handful of the guys—all in shorts and trim shirts—show up with different hair every week (red, hennaed, black, snow-white), though most of the more elegant types are always their smooth, smiling selves, bringing the manners of the executive floor to our daily battles.

After some weeks in their company, I'd begun to assign my new friends names so as to identify them when I come home with my stories. The tiny woman with short gray hair, who bestows grandmotherly kindness on one and all—as well as lightning penholder backhands—I dub "the Bodhisattva," for her air of generalized friendliness; one of the other matrons, with a broad face and a constant smile, though a slight air of haplessness at the table, Hiroko, with her unfailing gift for these things, calls "Charlie Brown." The man who will become our chairman when we form a guerrilla group—he must be a dentist, I somehow decide—has only two expressions: no expression at all and a quiet chuckle. They play off each other powerfully, as sunny days and rain.

Two women in their late fifties who are always gossiping in the corner I cast as the Wyrd Sisters; the one who never reaches for balls and has a lazy air of command—I imagine a lot of gold jewelry and a slow-moving Benz—questions me so often on what I do for a living, who my wife is, why we're here, that I decide it's a very good time to know no Japanese at all. Her companion-in-arms, sometimes dressed in a purple T-shirt that says "Make an Enemy," has a tall beehive cut out of *The Flintstones,* severe glasses and a somewhat ferocious air.

But as soon as we're rallying together, she's all furious concentration, and capable of hitting the ball at terrifying speeds while staring down at it as if hypnotized. She becomes the first to call me "Pico-chan," the affectionate diminutive extended to children and pets.

One day her husband appears, an extraordinarily friendly soul with a constant smile. He seems to specialize in two words of English, "happy" and "retire."

"How are you?" I ask him in Japanese.

"Happy," he says, in my language, though his face broadcasts it even more. "Retire!"

"No work, eh?"

"No. Always happy now. Retire."

He's the first one to invite me to coffee and a chat after the game.

For so long in Japan, the local men seemed a kind of alien species impossible to get close to. Women were always welcoming; everyone from the older ladies in shops, who spoke to me in crystalline Japanese, patient and kindly, to the young girls at cash registers, deliberately chirpy and full of professional smiles, did everything they could to make communication possible. They were glad, I could imagine, of the real-life adventure movie and escape hatch a foreigner presents. Most men, however, wanted to have nothing to do with me. I saw them brusquely ordering around workers in the convenience stores, with never a word of thanks. Lecturing kids on their behavior in the bus. Under such pressure with their long commutes to unforgiving jobs that they often seemed to acknowledge no public emotion at all.

Now, though, set loose in a gaggle of mostly retired men, I get to see them on a weekend perpetual. Mr. Kyoto, as I think of him, is coltishly running across the floor to collect fallen balls, and roaring "Okayyy!" when one of his slams goes in. Someone else does a little dance when he hits a winner, unable to contain his pride and relief. I pass one of them in the locker room, and he flashes a shy smile and asks if I don't want to join them for golf. Allowed to be human again—their responsibility, formerly to protect their families by being away from them, is now to protect their families by being with them—they couldn't be more engaging.

The man with the gold tooth, in his Speedo-tight shorts with the lightning bolt across them—a strange complement to his shy accountant's manner and ill-at-ease boy's grin—happily greets me in the street and, proud that he knows the migratory habits of this odd bird, says, "Six months in America, right? To do your job and protect your mother? Six months here?"

"That's right."

A newcomer, when he picks a yarrow stick that allows him to play, while I get the one that obliges me to sit out a game, slips me his stick when no one's looking so that I get the chance not to miss a single game. I protest, and he says, "No, no, Pico-san. Please."

Another man, who can hit a backhand winner with a carelessly flipped wrist, I suddenly encounter one evening in his other face on a plane from Okinawa, impeccable in his dark suit, thirty seats ahead of us, in Business Class. Others come up as I'm on the treadmill and tap me on the shoulder so they can shake my hand.

Meanwhile, the Emperor and the Empress, perfectly groomed, canvass new players for our group, organize trips to tournaments across the area, make sure that everyone knows just enough about everyone else, but not too much. "Nice footwork," says the Emperor in English; his wife, with her scarlet headband and flashing eyes, says, "So cool, Pico-san! We missed your long serves while you were away."

On my birthday, this elegant woman with a beautiful forehand she's brought over from the tennis courts leads everyone in a chorus of "Happy birthday, dear Pico." And every time I return—five times a week—she greets me, with typical sincerity, "Pico-san, how nice to see you. Have you been well?" Her husband clearly enjoys practicing his boardroom English with me, and one time, with a crinkly smile, offers, "You know John Deere tractor? I went to their factory in St Louis. And board meetings. Chicago, Memphis, everywhere. Forty years, work, work, work. No fun!"

One day the good-natured man with the moon face— I'd taken him to be my age until he told me he was seventy-nine—comes up as I catch my breath between games and says, "Excuse me, Pico-san. I have a question."

"Of course."

"Is it 'a practice difficult to deal with'"—he pulls out a little notebook—"or 'a difficult practice to deal with'"?

No wonder I so often feel out of my depth in Japan.

"I think both are okay."

"Really? Both?"

"No problem."

"Thank you, Pico-san," he says and goes back to dancing around the table in his spiffy new Air Jordans and running happily after every ball that flies off.

"You're well?" I ask friendly Mr. Joy, standing almost at the wall as he patiently hits easy balls back to a woman who swings wildly at every one and smashes them into the net.

"Always happy," he says in English. "Old Power!" Then he remembers something, "Ah, Pico-san, just a minute."

He hurries across the room and rummages through his bag, extracting at last an elaborate catalogue from an exhibition of European paintings. From Osaka, I notice, in 1974.

He hands it over, and I page through it slowly, admiring Monets and Renoirs, then hand it back.

"No, no, Pico-san. I want you to keep it!"

"You don't need it?"

"No! I'm going through my things—we're moving house—and I found this. So I thought of you."

"But your grandchildren . . . ?"

"Please, enjoy it."

Then he goes back to the table and invites the matron to keep practicing.

By the time I walk home, I can just make out one small, silent figure—Mr. Gold Tooth—shuffling his slow way home, alone. The season of separations is drawing on.

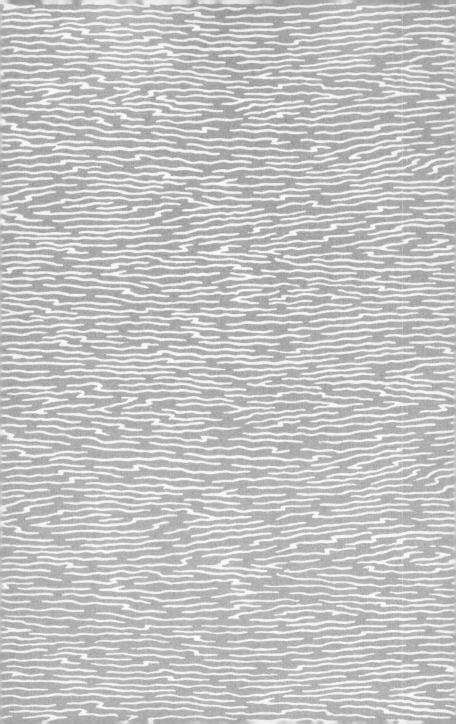

II

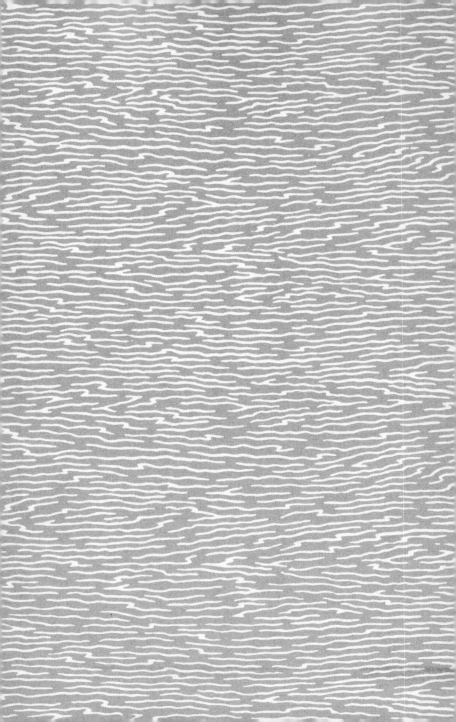

"I think I could write a poem to be called 'Concord,'"
Thoreau wrote one early autumn, when he was twenty-four.
"For argument I should have the River, the Woods, the Ponds,
the Hills, the Fields, the Swamps and Meadows, the Streets
and Buildings, and the Villagers. Then Morning, Noon, and
Evening, Spring, Summer, Autumn, and Winter, Night,
Indian Summer, and the Mountains in the Horizon."

The days feel so newly minted as the mildness of early October gives a frame to the blue, I hardly notice I'm walking through a landscape of decay. The same landscape, in truth, that moved the Buddha to leave his gilded palace at the age of twenty-nine and try to find out how to make his peace with old age, suffering and death. I take the long walk out of our suburb and up the hill to the new shopping center next to the health club—I need to buy a cartridge for our printer—and as I step into the vast electronics store on the third floor, it's to find all the sofas in front of its sixty-five-inch plasma screens fully occupied.

An elderly couple is on one; a wisp-haired senior citizen occupies another. Slumped around the third, two old men are watching Tigers highlights as if seated together at the ball-park. How much better, they've clearly decided, to watch TV all day in a public place—brightly lit, full of faces, with diversion all around—than in an empty room at home.

My next stop is the town's main library, and when I get out of the bus, it's to walk into four old men jockeying for position at the front doors. It's 9:25, and each is angling to be the first to race in when the doors slide open, five minutes from now, and grab today's copy of the *Mainichi Shimbun* and the carrel next to the window.

I know there's no hope for me in this battle, so I take a ten-minute walk, past a new forest of softly lit condos, up to our most lavish local train station, and visit McDonald's on the second floor. Almost all its fifteen tables are taken; at every one sits a very elderly gent, newspaper laid out on the Formica table in front of him, or book in hand, a single straw poking through the lid of his paper cup.

I claim a place, the last piece in the puzzle, and wonder if the others are going to be here all day, till their granddaughters spill in at 3:00 p.m.—a flurry of high-pitched squeals and pink handbags—and turn the place into an after-hours study hall. And then, as I join the abandoned elders, suddenly I recall the flight I'd taken over here four days after my father-in-law's death. Scanning the offers on the video monitor, I'd been surprised to see the classic film by Yasujiro Ozu, *Tokyo Story*, available, sixty years after its release.

I'd turned it on, pulling down a shutter to close out the blue sky above the Pacific, and very quickly I was with an elderly man and woman just after the war, as they visited their children in their busy lives in Tokyo. The age-old Japanese theme of torn responsibilities, but given new force now that the young generation is in the city, working to rebuild its country, even as its parents belong to a rural order that seems to be on its way out. In a central scene, played out almost silently, the couple's son, who's promised to take his parents out on an exciting excursion to a department store, is interrupted, just as they're heading off, by a neighbor: a boy nearby has come down with a fever; the doctor son has to attend to his professional duties, and his parents trudge upstairs again and change out of their Sunday finest, to spend the day alone.

As I returned to the familiar story on this occasion, though, I realized I was following a shadow tale, much closer to home. The elderly couple came—I'd never noticed before—from Onomichi, the same small town not far from Hiroshima that my now late father-in-law claimed as his home. They spoke in the Hiroshima dialect that was his. Trains kept rattling through the black-and-white landscape, a symbol of how families were scattering in the postwar world, and people were always ready to move away, and to leave loved ones behind. I might have been sitting on the tatami around my in-laws' low table as Ozu's camera, always in the same low position, silently looks up at faces newly alone as the seasons turn.

When three old men gather for a drink in the film, one of them complains that his son is no more attentive than a lodger would be. Another looks almost envious: his two sons are gone, casualties of war. The elderly mother calls out to her grandsons, but both little boys run away; the unhoused grandparents end up taking a quiet picnic beside a graveyard. The only one who greets them with warm cries of "Mother! Father!"—as fresh as April—turns out to be their daughter-in-law, free mostly because her husband, the couple's son, was lost to war eight years before.

The plane touched down in Narita, and I walked out into the soft buzz of the terminal, crowded with spiky black heels and girls in fishnet stockings poring over smartphones and walking smartly out into the brisk blue. For many minutes, though, I was still with the elderly couple onscreen, being shunted, like lost luggage, from one house to another.

"Life is disappointing, isn't it?" says a young girl who's just lost her mother, near the movie's end.

Her sister-in-law, only slightly older but a widow already, breaks into a radiant smile. "Yes," she says, in the voice of classical Japan. "It is."

Now, on another "baby spring" day—there's a strikingly Japanese absence of aggression and loudness in the air—I head up the hill again, past the new storage sheds and the old gas station, past the Paris hair salon and the Family Mart convenience store, through the Slope of Light suburb. The complex in which the Renaissance health club sits is distilled essence of modern Japan. Until six years ago, it was just rolling hills, like the ones we can see in every direction. The trees blazed and reddened in November; sheep grazed—as they still do—in the grassy area above what is now a long, spooky flight of steps, across from the fresh shopping center that calls itself "Life."

But postwar Japan is the story of the triumph of concrete over wood—Man's designs over Nature's—and so this virgin stretch proved too tempting to leave alone. A subway station, linking us to almost five hundred other stations around western Japan, came up in the wilderness. Next to it is that sprawling three-story big-box shopping center, with an Aeon outlet—the local Costco—overseeing Ronald McDonald and Colonel Sanders and other commanders from the Mall of America. "You know," wrote a Japanese friend of mine in Tokyo who delights in chronicling the dissolution of old Japan, "that crime rates soar whenever there's an Aeon in the neighborhood?" A sign, he suggests, of being in neither city nor countryside, but just suburban Nowhereland.

In the studio today, Mr. Gold Tooth is already getting ready to leave, pouring oil on his paddle and stashing it between sheets of transparent plastic before placing it within a cover; he's told me with pride how he spent $250 on it. My tall and stately friend who speaks perfect English, the picture of athletic cool in his blazing orange T-shirt (he's about to turn eighty), is coming in with his trim, ponytailed, constantly gracious wife and telling me how they'd just gone into central Nara to get new rubber for their rackets—only sixty dollars (every month). I look at the eighteen-dollar bat I bought in a department store and am reminded how different I still am from my passionate hobbyist friends; they're waggling a finger under the table, like Olympians, to show partners how they're planning to serve, while I'm trying to unriddle my piece for *The New York Review of Books* on the warlords of Mogadishu.

It's almost dark by the time I get home, and as the days begin to shorten, and night comes ever earlier, I can see Hiroko going back, again and again, to the mystery that encircles us.

"One time," she says, as she demolishes some eggs in a wooden box while I eat the broccoli and cabbage she's kindly cooked for me, "my brother telling me he must do some test. With his friend."

I stop eating; it's not often Hiroko has told me about her

brother's professional life. It's almost as much a closed book to her as it is to me.

"That time, little they showing children many picture. Then ask: 'Which face happy? Which face calm? Which person you think beautiful?'

"One boy, he every answer perfect. So intelligent! Every answer correct. But then my brother show him two picture—'Which one beautiful?' And this boy choose one with very strange face. Not so gorgeous.

"They so surprise! Little shock feeling. Then, test-finish time, boy's mother coming, take him home. She look exactly same face, so strange."

She smiles back up at me. "Every kid, mother's face so beautiful!"

As autumn seeps into my spirit—I'm beginning to lose track of what is it and what me—I feel as if I'm starting to disappear. My sentences grow slower, bodiless; the hyper, super-sensory teenager who got off the plane in an adrenaline rush is settling into a rhythm, and growing harder and harder to discern. Last December, when a visitor took a picture of us, Hiroko and I pored over the result, barely able to see the nearly invisible ghost that was me, almost part of the furniture in the background. Then I flew back to California, and the whole process was reversed again, as if rewound at sixteen times normal speed, and I became a high-pitched adolescent once more, ready to speed through the seven ages of man again in the next seven weeks.

Very early today, Hiroko is out of her bed, ringing a bell beside her homemade altar, and placing sweet tangerines in front of her four Buddha statues, her cat's-eye rosary in a green velvet bag, a spray of fresh lilies in a vase behind them, her Tibetan prayer wheel. As I come to consciousness, she's waving incense all around, as in a church, and throwing open every window to the predawn chill—the way we'll fling out roasted soybeans in early February, crying, "Devil, go out! Happiness, stay in!" Then—dread moment—she puts on a recording of low-voiced Tibetan chants, and sits stock-still for twenty minutes, before hauling every spare piece of clothing she can find into the washing machine and whipping up (in eight minutes or less) tonight's dinner.

This from the woman who runs out of the room, hands clamped to her ears, whenever I put on Leonard Cohen, because he sounds too much like the Buddhist funeral chants she heard all around her as a girl amidst the temples of southern Kyoto.

Her kids and I tease her remorselessly about her devotion to cleaning, but of course it's Hiroko's deeper cleanliness—her freedom from second thoughts, from the need to gossip, from malice or the hunger for complexity—that is one of her sovereign gifts. Dusting is how she clears her head. Cohen himself, asked about his Zen training, explained, "It's just house cleaning. From time to time the dust and the dirty clothes accumulate in the corners and it's time to clean up."

Today, after she completes her ritual, she starts riffling

through drawers and then takes a seat at the dinner table, above scattered sheets of pink writing paper, cherry blossoms fluttering along their sides.

"Isn't this the day for your tai chi class?" I call from the bed, four feet away.

"Soon," comes the distracted answer. "First, I little write letter."

"Who to?"

"My brother."

She's silent for a long time, and I think of all the hours she spends sending the absent Masahiro birthday greetings or postcards, assurances that all is well.

When she gets up, I ask what she wrote.

"Same. Always same. Our mother not so young. Doctor say her heart not usual size. Double. Any moment, she can die. He still our blood, member our family. Cannot erase." She stops. "Always my brother and my mother so close. Her dream, all life live together my brother."

"I hope he listens."

"I hope, too."

"My mother so weak now," she goes on. "Always she asking, 'Where my son? He die?'"

"'No, mother, he here.' Then so confused. Because he never there."

"I'm proud of you," I say, getting up. "Please, keep writing. Even if he doesn't answer, none of it is wasted."

"I try."

She tells him not to worry about her, she has a happy life.

Her children are happy and healthy, and they feel she chose well, the second time, in love. He'd be surprised if he could see how comfortable she is abroad.

She doesn't want or expect anything from him, she writes. But if he could spare a thought for their mother . . .

She folds the paper, very carefully—in shops sometimes, she asks the woman behind the counter if she can do the wrapping—and puts it in the flower-decorated envelope, flipping through her address book to find out where he lives.

Then she's out into our two-square-foot entrance hall, and wrestling on her boots. Sunglasses on, she speeds to the bus stop to go for a day's ghostlike movements in the park.

It's raining when I wake up. The buses are grinding their gears on the road outside, and darkness has lifted, but still no light is coming through our heavy, frosted-glass doors. I pull them back and see water puddling on the roof of the post office across the way, pattering down on the few parked cars that are visible, streaming in one unceasing torrent down on the young girl who's tottering on four-inch heels to the bus stop, struggling to hold purse and shopping bag and open umbrella all at once.

Autumn is the season of subtractions, the Japanese art of taking more and more away to charge the few things that remain. At least four times as many classical poems are set in autumn and spring, the seasons of transition, than in summer and winter. But what that means, I realize as the years pass, is that nothing can be taken for granted; people are on alert, wide awake, ready to seize each day as a blessing because the next one can't be counted on.

And, in the luxury of our shrinking and uncluttered days, I recall why I was so glad of an empty room when I left my crowded life back in New York City; as Hiroko tells me stories from her girlhood before breakfast now, I give myself to her entirely, for as long as she speaks, with nothing else to carry me away. She does the same in return. There's no car to take in for a smog test this afternoon, no "breaking news" banner perpetually scrolling across a screen from CNN, telling us what we already knew six months ago. I take my watch off the minute I arrive in Deer's Slope—I'll never have to be anywhere at 3:00 p.m.—and when I pull back the door to the terrace and walk out for an hour with a book and a cup of tea, I feel as if "rush" and "distraction" are words in a foreign lexicon. "To learn something new"—a wise friend from New York sent me the sentence from John Burroughs last week—"take the path that you took yesterday."

"I small time," Hiroko says now as the world outside our window gets erased in the seeping gray and the rain beats down on the little lane, "always I little thinking about death. What it mean? Where we go?"

"That's so strange. That's usually the time we're thinking of nothing at all."

"Your life so different! Every time my mother little asthma problem. Cannot breathe. Always hospital. My father, too. So many operation."

"You learned about autumn early."

"One time only, my father hold me. That time, my mother hospital. I thinking, 'Maybe she never come back. Maybe I never see her again.' I cry."

"You never cry."

"Yes. That time only. My father come, hold me."

"How about your brother?"

"We don't know anything. So small. My brother, too, always sick." She's told me how, even when healthy, he spent all his time in his room, with his books, behind a sign that said "No Entrance. Especially to Hiroko."

"Always that time," she goes on, "people coming to our house."

"Friends?"

"No! Religion group! They want to pray. They know my mother sick, so they come. 'Something in your house wrong,' they say. 'We can help.'

"One time they burn everything. 'You must burn these things. This is poison in your house. In your heart.' That time, my father come back, he crazy angry! 'You are going to hell!'"

Outside, we can hear kids scuffling off to school. The buses stop, a few yards away from our window, and then start up again, more frequent in the early morning. The rain comes down on cars and gray tile roofs.

"Same when Sachi hospital. You no remember? Maybe Takashi little tell friend. Then always these group calling our house. 'You need help. Join us.'"

She has no time for such interventions. And yet, I think, Hiroko is always talking of "God." I can't imagine she's got a white-bearded man in mind, but I don't know what exactly she does see: her whole country is for her a teeming network of chattering crickets and tutelary spirits and heavenly forces she has to appease and watch closely, as she might a boss. When I called from Marrakesh to say that I felt darkness everywhere, she told me to put salt in my pocket.

"How am I going to get salt?"

"Please, try room service. Please. Order food, then they bring salt. Not so difficult."

Whenever something good happens, she says, "God little give you prize. You good person, so you win lottery." And if circumstances turn bad, that means I'm terrible and have brought on the bad future?

When she gets out of bed this morning, and buttons herself up into an elegant black raincoat and dons a navy-blue beret—being with her has taught fashion-allergic me to notice such things—she comes to where I'm sitting and speedily scribbles some characters across my back with her finger, then blows on them as if to make them stay. An impromptu Hiroko blessing, to protect me from all evil, copying a little of the Heart Sutra onto my spine before she puts on her shades and struggles into her tall black boots.

. . .

When Masahiro decided to cut off from his family—perhaps he needed to give reason to what was simple, human impatience—he sent a long letter to his parents, another to Hiroko; he might have been bringing the modern therapeutic way of settling accounts to an old society that thrives by stepping around conflict and allowing the seasons to sort everything out. I never forget the day when Hiroko, during her day's cleaning, found a cassette marked *Edward Scissorhands* under the bed of our thoughtful and bighearted son, then in his teens. With unabashed excitement, she thrust it into the VCR player—she could never get enough of Johnny Depp—only to find scenes from a much racier kind of movie begin to unreel before her. Boys will be boys, she thought as she flung the disappointing tape into a giant white garbage bag to be left out on the street.

A few hours later, our son came back from school and at some point no doubt registered that his tape was gone. As silently as his mother, he replaced it, I presume; boys will be boys, he surely felt. Both passed through what can be a turbulent phase of shouting and confrontation with a grown-up sense of what reality is and what their place in it might be, never needing to exchange a word.

But Masahiro seems to be convinced that boys should be something more than boys. He's importing a vision of perfection into a cyclical order that turns around the knowledge that everything is mortal. I'm not sure psychology, and looking for the human cause for all our suffering, can work in a place that flourishes on not looking for answers and ascribing difficulty to something in the heavens.

"Maybe I wrong," says Hiroko, as she remembers the pivotal moment. "I not perfect, I know. I many mistake. But my parent so old. He writing twenty page, telling everything they wrong."

The kind of letter shrinks advise their patients to write, but never to send.

"Me, too," she says. "Such a long letter. Not wrong. What he say true. I cannot usual Japanese life, I always little balloon; I need more ground. But now too late. We cannot change past."

I don't need to remind her that it was her brother who told her, when they were young, that they could blame anything until the age of twenty on their parents; after that date of official adulthood, they had to take responsibility themselves.

"Maybe . . ."

"Sometimes," she goes on, "I watching my son . . ." And she doesn't need to say more, since every parent is found guilty before the jury of her children—until, perhaps, those children become parents themselves.

We hear the wind outside blowing through the trees, the cars stopping and starting; soon the paths will be so full of fallen leaves we'll barely feel the ground beneath us.

"No word from your brother?" I ask three days later.

She barely bothers to answer.

"Why is it, do you think? How can he . . ."

And then I stop. I see myself at fourteen, nineteen, twenty-six, walking through my father's room while visiting my parents' home in California. Usually, my charismatic, wildly mischievous father is sitting in his blue chair, the cat by his side, reading a book and looking up, eyes alight with pride, as his only child walks past.

He says something fond or admiring, to me—or about me to whichever student happens to be there—and I smile politely and walk through without a word, freezing them out with courtesy.

Outside, it's still gray. The Japanese love the word *naga-ame,* for the long rains of winter, the sound itself conveying extended hours by the window waiting for the skies to clear.

That night, in my sleep, I feel Hiroko shaking me awake. I fumble around, and see from the clock it's after midnight.

"What is it? What's happening?"

"I see dream, my father," she says. "I'm sorry. Your friend there. One bus driver. We need money. I talking father, telephone. But he not know he dead. So I must pretend he alive. I so careful; I cannot say anything he understand dead.

"Then telephone stop. He not say anything."

She pauses and says nothing for a while.

"That means he gone. He knows."

I hold her close, and we listen to the rain, still coming down outside. The hiss of tires, the occasional gasp of water that deepens the silence of a Japanese garden.

"I miss my father," says Hiroko. "But so much I feel I talking him. So natural. Just like every time. I trying so careful in my dream.

"Then telephone stop. So sudden."

I hold her till she sleeps.

In the morning, when I wake up, I notice that my wife is wearing not one of her elegant, thin silver-bracelet watches, to go with her diamond earrings, but a more chunky silver number.

"You no catch?" she says when I mention it.

I shake my head; professional observer, I'm expert at failing to observe anything important.

"He want to give you; you no remember?"

Not quite. More than once, when we visited, her father would eagerly make me some of his special green tea, then hurry off upstairs to burrow in the closets of the tiny house for a set of silver medals he'd been given on retirement after thirty years of service to the post-office bank.

I didn't know what to say when he handed them over to me.

"You should keep these," I tried to respond. "They mean so much."

"No, no, I want you to have them."

So generous in one way, but poignant, too: he had no one

but a son-in-law whom he barely knew on whom to bestow his proudest possession.

Another time, it was the watch.

"When I go hospital last time," Hiroko says, "I get everything he like. To take to him."

"In case . . ."

She nods. "And now I feel—not exactly guilty. But sad. Maybe I shouldn't." She falters. "Maybe I little waiting my father die."

"You were trying to bring him back. By showing him all the things he loved."

She nods, and looks away. "I know." The voice shakes. "I know what you are saying. But . . ."

This evening, when she comes back from her job, Hiroko unpacks an anthology of stories, from her colleagues and her customers. As usual, they're of the autumn hiding behind midsummer. When I visit her at work, I walk through a gallery of brightly smiling, perfectly lipsticked, chirping young women, a light in their eyes as they deliver sincerest greetings. But Hiroko, of course, spends much of her life backstage. That young woman who professed a love of Joseph Gordon-Levitt left her diary out for everyone to see, and in it her friends could read, "I don't trust a soul!" That other one, so full of guileless cheer in her sixties, has a secret boyfriend. This one has a mobster father who looks out for her, and that one, so ladylike in cardigan and pearls, called Hiroko in the dead of night after burying a kitchen knife in her two-timing husband's thigh.

The sweetest and brightest of them all, time after time, had asked Hiroko to join her one evening for dinner. We soon learned why: in her mid-forties, with two high-school sons at home, she'd grown fascinated with a young musician whose concerts she'd been attending. Should she throw everything over and join him?

Hiroko, a pioneer in remaking her life by walking out of a marriage that was wrong for her, listens politely, and asks her friend if she's thought it through; indigo lasts longer than love, as the old Japanese axiom has it, turning on the fact that the two words are homonyms in her language.

She feels happy with the rock star, her friend says; she feels young again, alive. Back to the person she'd feared she'd lost.

And then, one day, as Hiroko drops her large bag on a chair and starts to take out the food she's brought home for dinner, she tells me how her cheerful friend's husband—we were going to have dinner together, to discuss our shared love of Raymond Chandler—has been diagnosed with cancer. Only a few weeks to live.

The next thing I know, the man is gone, and his wife is buying a cake for a dead man's birthday, listening again and again to his voice on the answering machine, remembering how handsome and attentive he always was, a star in his fancy company and her love since college time.

The musician's still there, Hiroko assures me, but as an

admonition, now. The opening her friend turned away from, too late.

It's bright and sharp again as I walk past a group of elderly vigilantes up the hill to the health club. I stop outside the sign (in English) for "Murakami Juridical Scrivener Office" to record in my little white notebook some thought before it flies away. I'm writing an essay on the weather now, it seems such a perfect reflection of the mind: a clouded day can make everything look bleak, even though the blue has never gone away; it's just obscured.

Part of the special joy of ping-pong here, of course, is that I don't have to clutter my mind with irrelevant knowledge about my friends: I don't know exactly what Mr. Joy did for a living, or what kind of household awaits Mrs. Endo after we're done (even if she's "Miss Endo"); my friends are likewise freed from all that extraneous stuff with me. I feel I know almost everything about the essence of each one of them, her station in life, her level of refinement, her readiness to work with everyone else; I know who tries always to cadge an extra game, who volunteers to play with weaker players, who will always cry out "six-four," when actually it's 5-5.

They know, in turn, my strange ways, and how I always wear worn jeans, add needless commentary to each point, look confused when rock-paper-scissors is replaced by another version that has no scissors, then head home before the rest of them.

All the surface stuff—salary, place of education, the implication of an address—falls away; we're left instead with some irreducible human reality that exists before and beyond all data, and with an appropriate sense of all we don't and cannot know.

One day, not long ago, I was walking to the post office when I passed the tiny woman with wire-rim specs and a tumble of gray hair whom I thought of as "the Bodhisattva," for her unhardened innocence and good nature, which sometimes expressed itself in a friendly lack of tact. "How many years did you say separate you?" she once asked the pretty young woman with the much older husband.

That day, to my surprise, she was with her equally pint-sized husband; they looked like a hobbit couple, though the husband, who'd always seemed a bit ill-at-ease with me, was not walking ahead of her, as most Japanese men of their generation do.

"How are you?" I asked brightly. "It's so beautiful today!"

She looked into the distance, saying nothing.

I remembered, too late, that she hadn't been well.

"How's your dog?"

She brightened visibly and said, "Very well."

Then, as before, she said, "You should come to the community center, Pico-san. Some Thursday afternoon. It's really fun. We all dress in kimono. And we perform the tea ceremony. It's fun. Bring your wife."

"I will," I said. "I have things to do the next couple of

Thursdays, but I'll make it as soon as I can." I wasn't kidding; she'd asked so often, I was determined to make it happen.

But when I came back from the health club, not many days on, Hiroko told me that the Bodhisattva had looked in on us and in fact drunk tea with Hiroko, whom she'd taken to be a nurse.

"She came to say goodbye," Hiroko went on, and I realized all I hadn't heard in my friend's sentences. So happy not to live in the illusion of knowledge, I'd missed the most important fact of all.

Every year, on October 20, her father's birthday, Hiroko and I used to rent a car for six hours and take her father and mother on a drive into the hills. It always began as an ordeal: the roads were narrow, and it wasn't easy for me to gauge distances in an unfamiliar vehicle navigating the "wrong" side of the road. The little lane outside my in-laws' house with the sign for "Takeuchi Tobacco" above it was permanently thronged with sightseers ambling towards the fox shrine, and the gates to the railway next to it came down every few minutes as a train whizzed past. In my head, I could see them drawbridging down while I was midway, slicing the car in two.

There was never room to park outside the little house, so Hiroko had to race in and fetch her parents, often unprepared for the regular surprise, while the neighbors stole glances at us and whispered, "Don't they say Takeuchi-san's daughter married a foreigner? Someone strange? Isn't that why Takeuchi-san is bringing down her shutters? So we don't see him?"

But soon enough her father came out, in well-pressed black jacket and turtleneck, even in his nineties—this was where Hiroko got her sense of style—and, seeing me, bustled back into the house to collect some sachets of extra-special tea. "Thank you," he invariably said, pressing them into my hands, and then "Sorry" and "Thank you" even before he'd said hello.

And before much longer, we were driving along the Kamo River in the sun, and Hiroko's mother was singing the classic song "Autumn Leaves," about flashes of crimson and ocher across a water's surface.

I know we have to maintain the tradition this year, even if the person we're celebrating is not here, and marking his birthday after marking his death day makes only a kind of paradoxical Buddhist sense. We stop in front of the trim three-story nursing home where Hiroko's mother now lives—across from a Filipina bar—and press a bell. The doors slide open, and we hurry in; Hiroko straightens the shoes in the entrance area, reflexively, and calls out a bright "Hallo?"

A woman bustles out—"Hi! How are you? Isn't it a beautiful day?"—and when we get out of the elevator two floors up, it's to find Hiroko's mother chattering and playing cards at a long table with the other patients.

"Sumiko-san, look! Your daughter's here to see you."

We're not sure she recognizes us—or maybe she's delivering a pointed hint by pretending not to recognize us. "Sumiko-san," says a nurse. "Your daughter's come to take you out!

Stop complaining. You're so lucky to have a daughter nearby who comes to see you."

So nearby that she could be living with her, it's hard not to think. And a son even closer.

My mother-in-law, the picture of alertness and fun when talking to the other elders, takes on a sad look, and screws her face up into a mask of pain.

We wheel the old lady, draped in a blanket and hurriedly dressed in layers for the early-autumn morning, into the elevator, and down into the reception hall, then into the tiny Toyota "eco-car." We pull out onto a main street, and then we're driving along the broad street—"Riverside Drive," as it could be translated—that runs along the water, leading towards the blue hills to the north.

Trucks are honking at me, and I can't read the signs. None of us knows how to program the GPS, and Hiroko is crying, "Careful! You're too close to the edge!"

But my mother-in-law is singing again, as if all the years have fallen away.

"Oh, I was such a cute thing when I was little," she says. "Everybody used to say I was so adorable. So sweet. We used to find cats when Hiroko was a child." ("It never happened," Hiroko says to me quietly from the passenger seat. "It's all imagined.")

"I'm so happy!" exclaims the old lady as we turn off the main drag, leading through an upmarket area of drive-through McDonald's outlets and BMW showrooms, and begin to navigate the winding turns that lead to Mount Hiei.

The trees are already starting to turn up here, where there is snow on the ground much longer than in the plains; the blaze of leaves is intense as we look down on the bright, hazy city cradled between hills on three sides. On the other side of the mountain is the modern town built around the lake that shares its name with a lute.

"Oh, let's pray for a long life!" cries the eighty-six-year-old woman in the back. "Let's live till we're one hundred.

"When I was a girl," she goes on, "everyone said I was so cute. Where did you get such a pretty little girl?" they asked my mother. "Sumi-chan's so beautiful."

She breaks into song again, a song from the days just after the war ended. "'Don't you worry, little sister, don't you stop. Keep on moving, little sister, don't lose hope.'"

We drive around the miles of curves that encircle the celebrated temples here. Mount Hiei is renowned for the sacred space known as Enryakuji. I'd been visiting the site for years before I realized that "Enryakuji" is not, in fact, the name of any single structure; the whole mountain is the temple, a place of prayer and preparation. There were once more than three thousand buildings on this mountain, brooding over the capital below, and sons of the emperors came here for twelve years of ascetic training.

Handel's "Ombra mai fu" is playing on the sound system, and each turn affords another dizzying view of slopes beginning to rust and blush, four weeks before the conflagration fills the streets below. Blue sky, bluer sky, completely depthless. Occasionally, when the window is open, I can hear a solemn bell resounding between the trees, an eerie sound in this place of untamed forests and ancient temples revealed in sudden clearings.

Kyoto is a sophisticated modern metropolis, lavish with urbane excitements. But Mount Hiei is the solemn, beating heart beneath the shiny surfaces. We might be taking my octogenarian mother-in-law to the secret shrine of her adopted home.

On the way down, two hours of songs and blue skies behind us, signs along the winding road advising us to keep an eye out for bears, we come to a coffee-shop-style "family restaurant" where parking looks easy, and pull into the lot beside it. We walk in, and over to a booth, and push the button that summons a waitress.

Then, as Hiroko orders food for her mother and asks her what she wants to drink—my wife's a young mother again, as when I met her—suddenly her mother looks down and begins to sob.

"What is it, Grandma? You were singing just a minute ago. Aren't you enjoying our outing?"

"I remember coming here with Grandpa," says the old woman.

"Don't worry," says Hiroko, soothing a little one. "He's right next to you. Always at your side."

The old lady keeps crying and crying, and then the food arrives and she forgets and perks up.

As we drive down Riverside Drive again, past the wooden platforms that frame the river till November—great white herons stand on rocks in the middle, as they never did, Hiroko says, when she was a girl—my mother-in-law abruptly seems to remember where we're heading.

"Let's go back to our home," she says. "We can live there together."

I could set my watch by it; the rending complaint begins every time, about thirty minutes before we have to say good-bye. And who can blame her? Hiroko understands as well as anyone how bleak a nursing home can seem.

Understanding doesn't help, though.

"We're going home?" says her mother.

"To the nursing home," says Hiroko.

"No! I don't want to go to the nursing home. Are you saying I have to die there?"

"No, Grandma. You're going to live to be a hundred. You were just saying so."

"But why can't I go home? I have two children, they both live near Kyoto. Why do I have to be alone in a nursing home?"

"I have to work, Grandma. If I'm not there, who's going to look after you?"

She looks confused. "Where's Grandpa?"

"He died, Grandma. Don't you remember?"

"Oh yes, he died. On the tenth of the month. Of pneumonia."

"I think it helps that she doesn't understand," I tell Hiroko after we say goodbye to her mother. "Or perhaps tries not to understand. Or doesn't want to understand."

"Helps," says Hiroko. "But still it hurts my heart."

· · ·

I feel I'm walking into the Himalayas as I step out of our flat this morning. A sudden mist enshrouds our little lane, and there's a mountain enclosedness to everything, though in Nepal the trash would never be confined to a single compact square on the street corner. An old woman is patting down the green netting that covers the bags of garbage—to protect them from the crows, cawing on our terrace—and then she secures it with a brick set out for the purpose, and a large, full bottle of water. Another woman is padding past in her jammies with her bag of refuse; I suppress a smile, until I remember I'm in jammies, too. At the bus stop across the street, a young woman appears to be sleeping where she stands, one of those Japanese tricks the likes of me will never fathom.

As the sun emerges, the day begins to fill the blank spaces in. A man appears outside our tiny post office, with a tank of goldfish. (Yesterday, in the same spot, was a micro–farmers' market, including boxes of lettuce and apples.) Inside, old ladies are sitting and chatting on a bench, sipping some cordial the man selling things outside brings them, in paper cups, while the Filipina from the apartment above ours (a mobster's moll, we assume, deputed to look after his aging mother) chooses among gorgeous new lines of stamps featuring Buddhist mudras, "Tales of the Stars" and the uniformed teddy bear who serves as post-office mascot.

Of late, the young cadaver with the ashen, sharp-boned face who inherited the post office from his father—even this is a family business—is devoting most of his attention to the garden he's developing in the four-car parking lot beside the building, a makeshift net converting it into a kind of green-house. He potters around the gated entrance while a woman beats her rug in her backyard. Nighties and blouses thicken the terraces of the apartment blocks, and washing machines gurgle and spit. A mini-pickup, white, is inching through the neighborhood, while a recording of a female voice sings brightly, "TVs, personal computers, air-conditioning units, PlayStations. . . ." Space is so limited in Japan that people pay these collectors to take their valuables off them, to be replaced by a new one every few months, it seems to me.

As I carry my letter into the post office, I catch the sound of two women, around my age, chattering outside it. "You know the waiting list is three years, they say?" "Tell me about it! You feel terrible if you keep them at home, you feel guilty if you don't." "And this morning, when I tried to give her her pills . . ."

After I've dispatched my postcard to Amman—only four minutes are needed to figure this out—the young woman on duty (my regular partner in crime is not to be seen) hands me a bag of tissues, points out the special postal-issue Kit-Kats and gorgeous Hiroshige reproduction stamps issued for Inter-national Letter Writing Week, while I take in the huge stuffed rabbit in front of her post, the CDs on sale, the umbrellas that are for some reason on offer.

Outside, fourteen young mothers in one-piece dresses and leather trench coats are waiting for a yellow minivan to pick up their kindergartners, one of the women with a baby pouched against her chest, another with a little girl playing at her skirts. The post office is also where our community's main public phone booth stands, gleaming in its glass box.

"How was your mother?" I ask Hiroko, much later, as the day subsides and the streets begin to empty again. Today, as on so many days off, she's made the long trip to southern Kyoto, and, because the weather was mild, taken the old lady to the zoo. I know the feeling: my mother has begun to take such delight in videos of dogs and stories about kittens that I've put away the histories of philosophy and Iris Murdoch novels I used to give her and offer her cat cartoons instead.

My wife plunks down her shopping bags, her heavy purse, tonight's spring rolls—all the debris of a long day out.

"My mother not so good."

"She was asking why you can't live together?"

"Opposite. So calm!"

I pause to take this in. "Isn't calm what we want?"

"Too calm," clarifies Hiroko. "So happy. She talking about her hometown. Not yet wartime. Everyone so friendly, so kind my mother.

"One boy next door—first time she told me this—he really like my mother. Every day he say, 'Sumiko-san, Sumiko-san, where you are?' He talk her, over wall. He carry her book to school. Same my brother.

"First time she told me this; I never heard before.

"His parents sell fish. So sometime he little thief. He taking fish, give my mother."

She catches my puzzled expression.

"True or not, I don't know. But she really like this boy.

Then, one day—she high school, first grade—he say, 'Now I go war. You never see me again.'

"'Don't go!' she shout. And he say, 'I must. Okinawa. I never coming back. Please, you go Yasukuni Shrine—all dead soldier there. You can think of me.'"

"We all start going back, don't you think?" I say. As the years behind us grow so much richer than the years ahead.

"That time," Hiroko goes on, undistracted, "so many people believe war. They must die, help Japan. My mother thinking Emperor is god. Everybody shouting 'Banzai! Banzai!' But my mother call, 'Don't go! Don't go to war!' Then policeman hit her."

"Hit her?"

"She showed me. And she shouting, 'Everybody, this policeman hit me!'"

"It sounds like a dream."

"I don't know. Maybe she thinking about this boy all her life. I don't know."

Or maybe not thinking. I understand why Hiroko's worried: the full-life review usually comes just before a death.

"Sometimes she remembers things that never happened," I remind Hiroko. "You told me so."

"Yes. I don't know she telling me true or not. But I never know this story. One day, my mother little go Tokyo. Together my father. She talking this today. Then they go Yasukuni Shrine. Suddenly he say, 'Somebody behind us!' Joke only. He always so scary ghost story.

"But my mother not thinking ghost. She think this boy!"

"So many years later."

"This reason, she hate war. Not only her family lose everything. But this kind of memory."

That's why, perhaps, she still thinks of all foreigners as spies, and the Japanese women who spend time with them—notably her daughter—as pan-pan girls.

"Funny. It was your father who never had any interest in the Emperor. But he's the one who had to risk his life to protect him."

Or not so funny. My father-in-law's stories of war were the unchanging sound track of his household; his wife and daughter—surely his son as well—can recite from memory the story of how he got on a horse in the prisoner-of-war camp and his companions told him to get down, lest the enemy see him. The story of how the Russians initially approached his regiment in its hiding place, and said, "The war is over. You've got to come out now." Some of the Japanese soldiers took it to be a trick and, by refusing to surrender, lost their chance ever to come home again.

Yet now that he's gone, these stories are most of what Hiroko has of him, her solace. Now it's she, like someone in the time of Homer, who's reciting the old stories she got by heart of how some of his comrades in the war lost their mind, and even the ones who didn't could never sleep again.

"Always," she says, as the skies begin to turn blue through the thick glass door leading to our terrace, "my father tell us. They must shoot, everyone is shooting, every direction. He lucky, he never fight face-to-face. He kill someone, many people, he doesn't know. But, everywhere, dead body. Even people eat dead body, they so hungry.

"My father lucky. He never do that."

Or else, like his wife, he allowed stories to take the place of experience; even a perfect memory may be glad of some correction.

"Worst thing," says Hiroko, "is tunnel. You remember, even we little go autumn leaf, Arashiyama Parkway, my father so scared tunnel? Because, wartime, they must go there. So terrible smell. Everywhere dead body. Looks like balloon; so fat. But if they do not walk, they die."

"And, meanwhile, your mother back in Japan was eating sawdust—maybe rats—to try to survive."

"So terrible time," she says. "Even you cannot imagine. We go Laos, Cambodia, for you so exotic. Monkey eating bread in street, kids want candy. For me not so exotic. I grow up time, Japan look like that. So poor."

It's not the moment to tell her that the man in whose house I used to stay during short holidays from school could never stop talking about the atrocities of the Japanese in war; nothing the British soldiers saw in Germany could compare to that. A colleague of my father's when I was a boy cut off his own finger while interned in Japan during the war to shame his guards into giving their prisoners more food.

Outside, the moon has come up, fat and low above the rooftops; it's warm tonight, an autumn day out of a poem.

But Hiroko is very far away. "You remember last week, I

go parent house little check my father thing? I find magazine. Nineteen eighty-eight. All show Siberia."

Forty years after he got out of his prisoner-of-war camp, he was still revisiting Khabarovsk, where more than half a million Japanese died. Telling the same old stories, of which everyone grew tired, or which they wrote off as an aging man's hazy fictions.

When I go back to the ping-pong club today, I start to make the calculations. My tiny, intrepid friend in the black slacks, Mrs. Fukushima, is eighty-three. That means she was eleven when Japan entered the war, and probably had to join other young women in bayonet practice, using bamboo spears; in her teens, she may have had to get her protein eating worms and snakes, like the girls around her. Perhaps she even collected cyanide along with her rations, as others did, in case enemy soldiers drew too close.

Mr. Gold Tooth, so full of boyish giggles, kindly Mr. Joy, the one with the shy, soft smile, all were in their formative years when up to eighty thousand civilians were killed in two and a half hours during the firebombing of Tokyo, and two-fifths of the city went up in flames. Mr. Kyoto has told me how his family moved out of the old capital to a remote village in the hopes of being safe. Kyoto was spared bombs during the war, but they could not know that until it made no difference.

"When I arrived in Lichfield," he goes on, in his poised,

fluent English, speaking of the rural town in the British Midlands to which he was suddenly assigned by his Japanese company in 1963, "the exchange rate was a thousand and eight yen to a single pound. I never forget that. And I was the first foreigner from Asia in the whole town! A town of eighteen thousand—no Indians, no Pakistanis, no Chinese."

"People didn't know what to do with you."

"That's right."

"Were you happy to get posted there?"

"No," he says, and I recognize in the directness one souvenir he brought back from the West. "At that time," he goes on, "there wasn't even a Japanese restaurant in the whole of England. There was only one place where you could get Japanese food—the Japanese Club. But for that we had to go to London, a long drive."

"So you couldn't even get ingredients to cook the food you recognized?"

"Nothing. I didn't speak English—only 'This is a pen,' something like that. I didn't know the difference between Birmingham and Buckingham!"

"You learned by immersion."

"That's right." The wit and sense of irony that his twenty-six years there armed him with are never far away. "My only weapon was my youth."

Every now and then, a very slim, striking young woman, whose accent is pure Kensington, arrives in the health club and starts working out with straight-backed determination; it's his soignée daughter, with whom, my friend says, he still exchanges e-mails only in English. Now a senior purser for

Cathay Pacific Airlines, living in Hong Kong and making of her international background a glamorous new life, which her parents, perhaps, could never have imagined when young.

"I small time," says Hiroko, when I relay some of this, "you cannot imagine. Nothing there! Everything gone. War finish time, we always feel war. That time, nobody can think anything. Only idea: we must repair. Only think of country, hard work every day."

Everybody looked after everybody else's family, she goes on. "I do something naughty, neighbor house say, 'Hiroko-chan, you bad girl! You must say sorry!'" Even fifteen years after the war ended, desperation brought everyone together. The Americans to her were *oni*, or devils; she launched exploratory adventures around the American base with her six-year-old friend, and they tingled with the thought that if the devils saw them they would eat them.

"No TV," she says, "no video game. Only we play Nature." Her kindergarten had been an American training camp. The local Buddhist university had been turned into a site for the army. When, finally, a TV arrived in the neighborhood—her father, characteristically, was the first to spend his secret savings on this new contraption—everyone gathered around the machine every evening, to see the world.

Six-year-old Hiroko, convinced there must be someone inside this box to deliver all the lines, used to go round the back in search of the ghostly presence.

"We watching Tokyo Olympic, we see Abebe from Africa, we cannot believe. Looks like other planet coming to our country."

In those days, I recall, no Japanese was permitted to go abroad, unless on a diplomatic mission or (as in Mr. Kyoto's case) for business.

Next morning, before the sun comes up, she begins to talk again. I've opened something up in her, and I'm guessing she hasn't slept much for the memories.

"I elementary school, first grade, second grade, my aunt tell me, 'Such a terrible wind. Black wind.' Everywhere—all our hometown, Hiroshima, broken. Like end of world.

"Children are crying, 'Mother, mother!' Their skin hanging out—like piece of kimono. So my aunt pretend be their mother.

"But other people are crying, 'Give me water, give me water or I die!' But if my aunt give water, she know, they die. One second.

"So what she can do? 'I only young woman,' my aunt tell me. 'Twenty year old. All hospital, doctor gone.'

"She look little same daughter in *Tokyo Story*. Kind, but looks so scary. She working Hiroshima bomb come time. Very close. Later, everyone little laughing her; she cannot make baby. Many, many time try, but always baby die in stomach.

"My uncle, too. He working Army School. Safe. But when bomb arrive, he must check school. Later, everyone call him bum. He always so hard worker, but he cannot work. Everybody so angry him. Then he die, so young. They understand leukemia. So many people die after bomb.

"My cousin, too. So happy. They have wife, children. But then, suddenly, they dead. Not so old. Cancer."

It strikes me that I almost never hear about her cousins; her father had five brothers and sisters, but the aftereffects of war were such that Hiroko has only three cousins, all women, that I've heard of. She grew up in a world of absences.

As autumn begins to surround us—there's no ignoring now the first reddening in bushes, the cosmos flowers, the signs in trendy department stores crying, "Oh! Autumn"—we follow its prompts as clearly as if it were our conductor. We know there's no budging it or anticipating its moves; like every god, it holds us through caprice. When first I arrived in Japan, I noted how much, like every religion, the seasons were turned into big business; and now that Japan has one foot in the West, the shops are filled with notices for Halloween, Black Friday, Christmas. But still there's something hushed and reverent about the billboard I see in an elegant hotel in Kyoto, citing twenty-eight local temples, their leaves graded "Early Stage" or "Partial View" or "Best." It's less like a weather forecast than a listing of the day's services.

This year, as I go to look in on my mother-in-law, I carry with me what Hiroko recently explained: that the old woman, when young, had to blacken her face with charcoal, or rough stones, because she was told that if she met an American soldier he'd want to rape her. In truth, the soldiers who appeared startled everyone with their kindness and generosity, distributing bars of chocolates to kids who hadn't seen candy in years and carrying themselves with a Gary Cooper elegance that makes Hiroko tremble even now.

But it's hardly surprising that my mother-in-law bars her doors reflexively to foreigners; older men sometimes mutter rough insults if they see Hiroko with me in a train. Five years after the war ended, fourteen or more had to share a single bare room in Nagasaki, and every year till 1951, one hundred thousand people in that city died of tuberculosis, while others tried to scrape the last piece of meat out of leftover American tins.

I start to ask more pointed questions now when I return to the group at the health club, as I begin to see what lies behind the stories of visiting factories in Tijuana or that company excursion to Mombasa. These guys exploding in infectious laughter over a missed shot at deuce, and flashing their hands so that scissors cut paper, were among the ones who made the so-called Japanese miracle, rebuilding their country after the war in record time, so that, very soon, their kids could spend summers in Redondo Beach, their wives could take three-day trips to Fairbanks to catch the Northern Lights. They're the ones who bulldozed all the broken buildings to the ground so as to erect this gleaming, ultramodern spectacle. It's almost as if they constructed the airport runway that now allows their loved ones to fly away.

I think of our own family and see how the story is the same: my father-in-law, after seven years in war and twenty years working for the government, saves up enough to send his son off to America for graduate school. The result is that his son barely speaks to him again. Hiroko longs to get a foreign destiny for her daughter, and then the daughter's gone to Valladolid, scarcely seen by us for eight years. Japan opens up to the world, and then worries that the world is diluting Japan. The country's wealth is so established by now that the whole land seems to be crying out for direction and a fresh sense of purpose, while the elders chatter that their kids, in cargo pants and hip-hop dreads, look like they're in one of the more broken parts of L.A.

Japan, like Hiroko after her first marriage, has a gift for turning the page and embarking on a new destiny that stuns and humbles many of the rest of us. But its neighbors and former enemies ask how you can create a future based on such a selective view of the past, and how turning a blind eye allows you to come to terms with the problems you've caused. Nobody talks much about the war after all these years, and yet its signs, its implications haunt every neighborhood. Maybe that's the silence Masahiro, too, after spending time abroad, chafed against.

I serve a hard, long one into the corner, and Mrs. Fukushima, using her bat as a kind of flyswatter, thwacks it into the far corner, for another winner.

. . .

The streets are turning into a sea of orange and black. Pumpkins are everywhere, and the gaudy ads for "Pumpkin Spice Latte" outside Starbucks almost make us forget the fire festival held since the eighth century in a village north of Kyoto, the arrival of persimmons and grapes, the apple crispness of the sharp blue days of late October. In the deer park, the stags' antlers were ceremonially cut two weeks ago, and soon, every evening, all twelve hundred four-legged gods' messengers will retire to a special grove as soon as they hear Beethoven's "Ode to Joy" played on an ancient instrument; more than sixteen hundred shrines around the country, and the Emperor himself, are sending their first harvest of the season to the sun goddess at Ise, not far from us. Traditionally, October is the "month of no gods" (since the gods are all said to convene at a shrine in Izumo for matchmaking); this is the time when farmers used to bring in their scarecrows—often made in the shape of gods— and offer them rice and vegetables in return for their service.

One dizzyingly clear day—*akibare* is the almost onomatopoeic term my neighbors use for the chill that begins to penetrate us now, in early mornings and after dark—Hiroko returns from Kyoto with a memory.

"Everything okay in your house?"

"Okay. I find more, more thing from Switzerland. My brother such big smile, he come back from there. So happy return my mother home. I tell you about Swedish people, New Year time?"

"I don't think so."

"One year—so strange—Sweden couple come my parent house, say hello. Happy New Year. Usually never foreigner visit."

"Sweden?"

"Maybe my brother spy? He want see my parent, so he send agent."

"Swiss people, you mean?"

"Yes, Switzerland. They so kind couple, so friendly. Little can speak Japanese. All asking my parent they healthy, everything okay."

"It sounds like that story of Kurosawa and his favorite actor, Mifune. After sixteen films together, over thirty years, out of nowhere something came between them. But one time, years later, both of them were making films in neighboring lots at the studio. Both of them, people said, started peeping over the wall to see how their old friend was doing. Each missed the other unassuageably.

"Your brother might be thinking of you at least as much as all of you think of him. Maybe more."

I recall that Masahiro will be sixty next year; the daughters of his we've never met must be close to thirty. And I think of how our kids lost a set of grandparents, and an aunt, their father's sister, when Hiroko got a divorce; but they also lost their biological father. He sounds like a kind and nice enough man, but he's never once seen his friendly, loyal, more than charming kids in over twenty years of living down the street. His responsibilities lie elsewhere now, as Japan's cut-and-dried divisions have it.

And after Masahiro broke from the family, claiming that he was traumatized by his sister's divorce, Sachi and her brother lost their only uncle, too, their only cousins that we know about, their other aunt.

"No problem" says Sachi when I ask her about it, and I can believe she has successfully erased them from her mind; but with their grandfather gone, too, now—and a grandmother failing—I worry that a part of autumn will be with her and her brother even in their spring.

The phone starts ringing in the dead of night, and I fling myself up from the bed and race across the room, heart pounding. I fumble for the receiver in the dark, grab hold of it. A beep-beep-beep signals a canceled call or wrong number. I go back to bed, more slowly, and lie there, heart thumping against my rib cage like a grandfather clock striking the hour every second.

For many long minutes, I cannot go to sleep. I listen for the sound of a bus groaning outside our window—a sign that it's not yet midnight, and the last bus hasn't passed. Occasionally, I hear a single car pass through the avenue of ginkgoes, off on who knows what kind of assignation. Sometimes, on evenings like this, Hiroko, as attuned to the world around us as a creature of the forest, says, "Rain."

"Really?"

"You can't hear it?"

I turn on my side and try to will myself back into the dark.

My mother is so far away, in her big house alone on a ridge, two-thirds of the way up the mountains in Santa Barbara. She's stoical and patient, never once complains about the winds that rattle the doors and can sweep her off her feet as she's coming in from the car after a night at the movies; when she calls, she sometimes forgets to mention that she just found a scorpion near her toilet, and a tarantula—regular October visitors, when the rains begin—underneath her bed.

Fires sweep through the hills around her as the sundowner winds pick up, and just to get a carton of low-fat milk, or take her arthritic cat to the vet, she has to drive around mountain curves so precipitous that many of her friends are too frightened to visit.

I'll be with her a few weeks from now, and I try to spend as much time as I can with her and to draw out from her now all her vivid, magical recollections of going downstairs every day as a girl in Bombay to give chili peppers to a parrot, of getting lost in a blizzard in the Himalayas during the war. I've taken her on four cruises in the past four years—Tallinn, Ephesus, Alaska, St. Lucia—and I bought her a shiny new car two years ago. The seasons are one of the ways we remember that children become parents of their parents.

But I can never protect her from fires or the earth moving, from autumn. The shadow side of being lucky enough to spend time in a country of my choosing is that I have one mother who's eighty-six and in a nursing home here, and another who's eighty-two and living even more precariously, alone, on the far side of the Pacific.

. . .

Sachi and I are seated beside a narrow stream in the center of Kyoto, overhung by apple-colored leaves in the October sunshine. The light is knife-sharp on this crystal day; passing under the forbidding wooden gate of Nanzenji, one of the city's five great "mountains of Zen," we'd found ourselves in an intricate latticework of light and shadow, the sun making shifting shapes on the white walls, across the raked-sand garden, on the greening moss. The light so fresh and clarifying in the quiet morning—sharpness and dryness define the season—that we might be stepping into a brand-new world.

"Uekusa-san called yesterday, from the nursing home," says Sachi, more and more lustrous and slender as her pining advances—such a long time now waiting by the phone. "I think she wants to decide what to do with my grandma."

"How does your grandma seem to you?"

"She's getting slower."

"But she's always so happy when we see her. I wasn't sure she'd last long after your grandfather went."

"Yes, she's happy. But when she goes to the bathroom, it's difficult. Even though it's not so far."

Next to us, four young women, elegant in their black outfits and with sleek ponytails, glasses of sparkling wine in front of them, take the warm afternoon in a flutter of (uniquely Japanese) chatter and birdsong. It's seventy-five degrees today—a rich, deep blue—and old men are walking in short-sleeve shirts along the canal at the center of town, past us.

"Your mother thinks so much now about prayers and ghosts and old Japanese customs."

"How about you?"

"I don't know. More than I used to."

"So that means, maybe twenty years from now . . ."

"I don't know. You didn't grow up with such a strong sense of old Japanese traditions and beliefs."

"Hmm. Who knows . . . ?"

The brightly smiling waitress brings out a thin white plate on which is perfectly placed some persimmon sorbet, with a thin slice of persimmon on the top, and another plate, mixing a mango madeleine with grapefruit pie.

A grandfather sits along the grassy bank, casting a line into the water.

"What is the name of this restaurant?" asks Sachi.

"Au Temps Perdu. Does that mean anything to you?"

She shakes her head.

"Basically, it means El Regreso de Tiempo Perdido."

"A nice name."

"You never think about your uncle?" I ask. "You probably don't remember him."

"No," she says; she barely remembers her biological father anymore, she tells Hiroko.

"Masahiro was always so proud of you. His wife got jealous, I think, because he had a picture of you and your brother up above his desk in Switzerland."

"I don't remember," she says. Women walk past us, carrying parasols to protect themselves from the sun in the slatted light.

Then she adds, "So tasty, isn't it?" Her smile is guileless-ness itself, fresh and open; a part of me hopes she's acquired the Japanese gift for phasing out a past that can no longer be amended.

"You never think about your home?" asks Sachi, as we wan-der through the festival sunshine beside the stream; much of Kyoto seems to be pouring towards the hills today. It's almost as if summer has come back for a moment—to retrieve some-thing it forgot—and everyone is crowding round it, the way the women at the ping-pong club do after I return from a trip, crying, "Long time, no see!"

"This is my home," I say. "I've never felt more at home than here."

"I mean England," she goes on. She's had to suffer, as has her mother, from hearing me say, again and again, when the fields are very green in midsummer, or on a day of constant rain, "I'm back again! In the place I've been trying to get away from all my life."

"Hiroko says it's the only place you can't find exotic. The only one where you're never surprised. But now you take her there every summer."

"That's true. I suppose it's pulling me back, just as Japan's now claiming your mother." I look at the hills, a mosaic of faded colors under the razor-sharp blue. "I like being in

Oxford with her, because she can see it with such freshness. No memories or prejudices."

"Like you with Kyoto," says bright Sachi.

"Maybe."

I can't put a finger on it as I try to explain it to my daughter; maybe autumn is the season when we start to turn within, and forgotten moments begin to bob up to the surface. In any case, if I could put an explanation on it, I wouldn't believe it.

The women are chatting outside the post office, and the boys are heading back through the early dark with their satchels, in dark uniforms. There's a sense of settledness and continuity to the cycles here, as to the ones I grew up in; the menacing world seems very far away. That sense of childhood's protectedness mixed with childhood's excited sense of not knowing what's going to happen next: liberation from a sense of future.

"Sometimes," I tell Sachi, "when I come back from the ping-pong club, through the neighborhood, I can smell cooking from every other house. Which is the smell of family, of home. Even if it's not a home that can ever officially be mine."

"Is that the reason you don't learn more Japanese?"

"Not exactly. That's just laziness. But it's the reason I live here on a tourist visa. I don't want to pretend I know more than I do, or fully belong where I don't and never can."

"Hiroko says you're always laughing when you're in England. So it must be your true home."

"Maybe. But you need a sense of open space in life, something to offset the sense of the familiar."

The chill begins to come at 4:20 p.m. now, though the

flaming last thirty minutes of sun are a true magic hour in this season; the golden light slanting through the streets gilds everything it touches.

"Maybe you see Japan more happily, too?" I tell my bright-eyed daughter. "Now you've lived for eight years in Europe?"

The TV screens are filled with stories of old people in Japan who have to rent actresses to come and visit them on Sundays—to call out, "Hi, Mom and Pop, how are you?"—because their own daughters have moved abroad, or lost their appetite for filial piety. Teenagers now sit, shirts untucked, on the silver seats reserved for their elders on buses, and each young woman who manages to fashion a new life for herself by marrying a foreigner or by joining a foreign company is that much further from the part for which she was raised.

I think of the trains that keep running through *Tokyo Story*, rattling out of sight even when the characters who watch them cannot do the same. They speak for an age of movement in which parents give their children the freedom they never had, only to wonder why, in their sunset years, they're feeling so abandoned.

When the old couple in Ozu's film look in on their daughter in her workplace—the Ooh La La Beauty Parlor—the young woman explains to a colleague that they're "just friends from the countryside."

No heath, no storm, no explosions of rage in this version

of *Lear*. Things are as they are, and every year people go out and watch the autumn, because it's always the same, and always not.

I'm playing the club chair today, the amiable, poker-faced gent who chuckles every time he gets the days mixed up and who regularly announces the score as "All nine," only for his wife to remind him, "Father! It's seven-four!" He's a lot like the absentminded father in every Ozu film, harmless and engaging, but never quite to be counted on for knowing what's going on (for that, you have to look to sharp-eyed wife or aunt or daughter).

Get him behind the table, though, and his pleasant, easygoing demeanor becomes lethal. In nine years, I've never seen him register emotion, other than affability and amusement; but on every service return, he threatens to flip his paddle to wrong-foot me, and he eases up so well when playing against newcomers that one forgets he can twirl his penholder grip around and send a low ball over so fast that it's at the wall by the time I notice it.

He guides us all by saying almost nothing, and when he tries to be stern—"Remember to take good care of the three-star balls; they cost three dollars a pop"—he defuses his own authority by lapsing into apologetic smiles, the same ones he flashes when he skillfully allows a 9-1 lead to turn into 9-9. The studied vagueness—the trailing-off sentences—with which many of my neighbors speak puts those around them at ease, even as it usefully lulls one into forgetting how effective they can be.

Besides, we'd be lost without our leader. Last week, I went into the studio to find eight of my friends rallying furiously at two of the tables, while, at the third, a quartet of old guys not connected to our group shouted and laughed over their weekly thirty-minute session. As I watched, however, I noticed that my pals were getting more and more tired. Mrs. Tanizaki always likes cutting through practice to get to the fun of real games, a person after my heart. The moon-faced "Doctor" in his spectacles canters after stray balls following every single rally, never complaining, but he's past retirement age now, and he's beginning to sweat under his beaming exterior. I looked around and realized: Mrs. Kyoto was gone. The woman who effortlessly organizes us all with the skill of a hostess at a garden party, taking pains to include every last person and jollying everyone along with encouragements, was away, and no one knew how to function without her.

My friends kept on and on, rallying, even though nobody wanted to; if they were to stop, it seemed, nobody would know what to do. I think of the government in Beijing, so convinced that if strong leadership is missing, everything will fall apart; a Confucian group is only as strong as its commitment to a clear hierarchy.

Finally, Mrs. Tanizaki could take no more. "Shall we get out the trump cards?"

But no one knew where they were.

"Okay, let's play rock-paper-scissors to choose sides."

"But there are nine of us now. That's not going to work."

"That's right. Let's play *goopa*"—rock and paper only—"so we can eliminate someone."

"But Pico-san's just come. He ought to get to play. Especially since he has to leave before the rest of us."

"Good idea."

"But Pico-san hasn't had a chance to practice. Is that okay?"

"You don't mind, Pico-san?"

"Not at all."

"Please," a woman said at last, seeing where this was going—or not going. "I'm sitting this one out. Truly. I'm too tired. You'll all be doing me a favor if you take my place."

In the presence of an odd number, everyone was at odds. But now we had a solution—until a newly permed matron with an oddly lunging style walked in with a smile, eager for a game, and we were nine again. The greatest happiness of the greatest number is never so easy to achieve unless somebody—Mrs. Kyoto, the gods, just the autumn chill—takes the lead in putting us in our place.

Two days later, I'm reminded again what the season of interiors can do with us. In summer, it's easy to be caught up in the rites of open-air festivals and evenings watching the moon along the Kamo River; but now, pushed inwards, we're picking up pieces of the jigsaw puzzle of the past, especially as Hiroko keeps taking the long series of trains to Kyoto for the melancholy business of sifting through her parents' stuff.

She's always been one who loves to toss things out—it goes with her constant generation of new hobbies—and in her it speaks for a positive, forward-looking nature. But now, as she goes through her parents' lives, she says, "I find so many letter today. Always my brother writing to my father. Saying, 'Thank you, thank you. Thank you you give present! Thank you you send money!'

"We never knew."

"You mean, all the time your brother was in Switzerland, your father was helping to support him? Not only when he went to graduate school in Kansas?" She nods.

"And then, after he'd paid for him to go abroad for all those years, he saw his son come back and turn his back on him."

"Same you," she says. "Your father pay your time at college."

"You're right," I acknowledge, taken aback. There's never any questioning her quick lawyer's logic.

As she takes things out of her bag, the stories that come out are such a confounding mix of superstition and fact that I lose all bearings.

During the war, she tells me, her father's mother put out fresh rice for her son every day, and tea, even though he was thousands of miles away; since his other brothers were not tall enough, he was the only one of her six children to go to war.

"Bad luck he had to go to war," I say.

"Not so bad. That time, so many love Emperor, love Japan. If not go war, little embarrassed feeling."

One day, she tells me, her father's mother collected the miso soup she'd put on her homemade shrine and noticed no condensation on the lip. She shivered. It was almost as if the faraway son she was trying to support suddenly lacked the strength to breathe.

That very moment, Hiroko says, her father was close to death. But, out of nowhere, he felt a spirit close to him—his mother—offering him rice, and he got up and came back to life.

Such are the stories with which a family, or a country, sustains itself, perhaps. They come to sound like the classical Japanese folktales that Hiroko used to spin out to me when first we met. It's hard to know what's true or not, but only a few weeks ago I saw a daughter bring her mother back to life, when Hiroko came to her mother's bedside and got her to eat again.

"It's strange," I tell my wife. "By being in Siberia, your father managed to survive. If it hadn't been for that, he might have been in his hometown, in Hiroshima, in 1945. He might not have lived to ninety-one. You might not be here now."

"Strange," she agrees. "We cannot know so many thing."

And who knows why, but, as I watch her gather her sword and kit for tai chi, her regular meeting with a gaggle of fresh retirees, I recall a bright morning in California, three months ago, where we'd gone to look in on my mother and ease her through recovery from back surgery. Hiroko is always reborn in the fresh light of the West, and the land of taco shacks and tawny hills is reborn for me through her excitement; no one can appreciate endless summer so much as a visitor from the world of autumn.

One morning, I took her to a yoga center downtown, a place she'd never tried before, and then drove back to my desk to work. An hour later, the phone began to ring.

"I'm sorry," said a strange voice, "but I think you should come and collect your wife. She's not making any sense."

Her English often trips people up, I thought, as she tries to put the most elaborate feelings and ideas into a kind of Japanese syntax (while I, speaking Japanese, am so shy and reticent that I might as well be Japanese).

I made my leisurely way back to the large yellow converted church near a park and sauntered upstairs, to find Hiroko sitting on a bench, awaiting me.

She offered me a bright smile, and we walked downstairs.

"What happened?" she asked, as we went out to the car.

"Oh, nothing. The woman was worried you might be sick."

She smiled as I let her in. I took my place behind the wheel, and she said, "What happened?"

I looked at her; attention is one of her striking graces. "Nothing. They were just worried."

I turned the key, and we began moving between the white-walled lawyers' offices and Pilates parlors that sit at the heart of the sunlit resort town.

"What happened?"

I looked at her as if to say, "You're joking!"

And then she said, "How we get here?"

"You remember we were in Toronto last week, for my job?" Something in me was beginning to stir. "You went to Niagara Falls."

"Niagara?"

"You don't remember our trip last week?" Now I was getting worried.

"What happened?"

"You know where you are?"

"I know!"

She was the same bright-eyed, perky soul I collected every day from the gym. But our conversation was running off the tracks, and there seemed no way to get it back on them.

"What happened?" Hiroko then said again, and I pulled over beside our historic Spanish-style courthouse and raced over to a phone booth to call our doctor.

"I'm sorry," said his assistant. "He's just stepped out for lunch. Is it something I can help you with?"

I described how Hiroko seemed frozen in some way, and the voice at the other end said, "Go to the emergency room. Now. Right now. Don't waste a minute. You have one hour; they call it the 'golden hour.' It could be a stroke."

I got back in the car and accelerated towards the nearest hospital, gunning through a yellow light, barely halting at the stop signs. I stole a glance at the woman I'd known for twenty-six years, her smile and open face and excited eyes under her red headband. She looked just the way she always did. "You remember Bernie?" I said, and she smiled. "Yes. Of course!"

Then I sped towards the entrance to the emergency room, inwardly cursing as one blood-red sign after another led me around corner after corner until, at last, we arrived at the Cottage Hospital door that said "Trauma Center."

What if . . . and all the what-ifs came pouring down on me. If she was fine in every way but we could never talk again? If truly her memory was gone, and now we no longer had a past, anything to share? What if I, notoriously ham-handed, was left to care for an invalid for life? What if, in a moment, on a carefree morning, our life together had been erased?

We ran into the tiny, overcrowded room, and a woman handed me a clipboard and pen. I led Hiroko to a seat and scribbled down answers to all the questions: name, date of birth, marital status, home address.

Then we waited.

"What happened?" asked Hiroko.

"We just need to make sure you're fine," I said, trying to push down a rising sense of panic.

"What happened?"

"You remember me?"

"Of course!" She smiled broadly. "Why you ask that?"

Thirty minutes later, we were ushered into another room, where a doctor in his mid-fifties with a mop of curly black hair, noting my agitation, invited me to sit down. Then he put his fingers on Hiroko's temples.

"What's your name?" he asked, and she answered as if it was a silly question.

"What date is it?"

She looked confused, though she might have had trouble with the question in the best of circumstances.

He asked a few more simple questions, and then he turned to me. "She's speaking gibberish," he said.

Something stopped in me.

"Which is good. I'm ninety-nine percent sure that she has transient global amnesia. She won't remember this day ever again, and, most likely, she'll never have an episode again. There's nothing she needs to take for it, there's nothing we can do. Just stay close to her, right next to her, for the next twenty-four hours. When she wakes up tomorrow, she should be fine."

I stared at him, not speaking, as if he'd raised us from the dead.

"I'll take some tests to make absolutely sure. But I'm confident that's the case. I'd never experienced this till my mother got it. It comes to some people sometimes, for no reason. It shouldn't happen again."

"Isn't there anything I should do?" I couldn't believe a life could be turned around in an instant and put together again in another.

"Nothing. Was there anything different or unusual about what you did today?"

"No." And then I remembered. "Well, she did try a new yoga center she'd never been to before. But I don't think . . ."

"Yes," said the doctor, looking relieved. "That would do it." Maybe send the blood into her brain in some different way.

I led Hiroko out into the broad sunshine, and took her home to rest. Almost instantly, she fell into a deep sleep. When I prodded her awake for dinner, she started and stared at me in terror, as if not recognizing a thing.

"What happened?"

Next day, our lives picked up again, and the storm had passed through town. True to the doctor's assessment, she could not remember the day or the episode. I, of course, could not forget. It was like one of those drills they conduct in schools and hotels, to prepare you for a fire. Except that the sign of a really good dress rehearsal is that it truly feels like the end of everything you know.

III

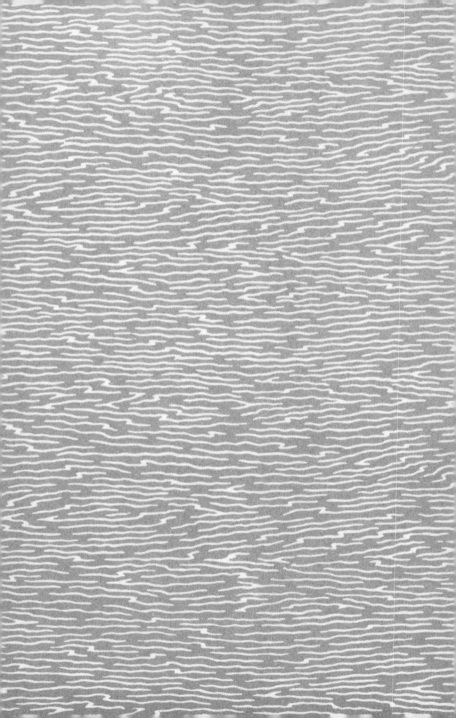

"I suppose everyone tries to ignore the passing of time,"
the very English poet Philip Larkin told The Paris Review
in 1982. "Some people by doing a lot, being in California one
year and Japan the next; or there's my way—making every
day and every year exactly the same. Probably neither works."

As November dawns, we step into a world of light. The whole room seems to pulse with smudged gold, as the sun rises above the hills beyond us and comes through the diffusing thick panes of our frosted-glass windows. I remember my surprise when Hiroko told me that the builder of this place, who ended up calling it "Memphis Apartments" in honor of Elvis, originally wanted to make it a church. The heavy pebbled glass spreads light as if it were incense.

Now she puts Bach on our system, and very soon the sun is making gold stripes across the terrace with such extravagance that I'm pulled in every direction all at once. A great rejoicing, so it feels, which awakens gratitude and delight; but the sun is passing across the terrace earlier and earlier, and by mid-afternoon it will disappear behind a roof.

It's nearly impossible to stay indoors on a day like this, not least because so many around me are being pulled, almost magnetically, out into the sharpened sunshine, to marvel at the fact that the sky is so blue even as the leaves rust and begin to flutter down. Many of Kyoto's temples open their gates after nightfall now—another of the city's fresh and ingenious seductions—

and soon we'll follow lanterns past stands of bamboo eerily lit up, watch fast-moving ghosts holographically projected upon raked-sand gardens. In the shallow crystal pond of Kodaiji, the five-pointed maples are almost more brilliant than on the trees that the temple's water reflects.

And yet, in our private lives, we're perched on the edge of a cliff, and the slightest movement could send us tumbling over. Every time I come back to the flat, I look, by instinct, for the green flashing button on the phone—no news is likely to be good news—and when I walk into the park, I can't help but wonder how often my mother-in-law will see the maples again. I take myself, to banish the thought, to Susano Shrine, where the light is slicing the courtyard into diamonds; and then I notice, as never before, that people have placed coins around rocks all across the forest, and there are stone lanterns everywhere, as if the whole wilderness were a haunted church.

I decide to take a train into central Nara today—I cannot squander this moment—and in the sun-washed carriage, I find myself looking at the hands on every side of me, tapping away on a smartphone, tightly gripping the handle of a designer bag, holding a toddler steady as the train rocks and rattles. The one part of Japan in which age cannot be concealed—hands tell the truth even when mouths and eyes cannot—is also the most beautiful.

In the deer park, an old woman has set herself on a bench, to transcribe the autumn colors in a sketchbook. Two toddlers are stumbling their way into learning to walk on the grass nearby. A deer is chasing some poor visitor into the store next to where special "deer cookies" are on sale for the equivalent of $1.50 each. If they are true messengers of the gods, the deer speak for gods as ungovernable as Zeus and Hera.

Around me there's a chorus—"Waaah, aren't the maples beautiful!"—and the chorus itself lends brightness to the day. A woman leads her dog, wrapped in a red blanket, up a slope and stops and tilts her head up, up, up, to where the leaves are picked out against the blue. "Quite something, no?" she says to her four-legged companion.

A young girl, in a denim jacket with frills, guides her grand-mother, very slowly, by the hand, then sets her down in front of the turning leaves, a classic autumn tableau. "Would you like . . . ?" a passing woman suggests, and the girl hands over her camera and hurries off to take her place next to the old lady.

"Now you?" asks the granddaughter, springing up.

Across the world, people are marking the Day of the Dead today, but in the park, the air so cleansed that the trees seem to gleam in the freshened morning, it's not skeletons I see so much as aging elders struggling for breath. Dying is the art we have to master, it seems to say—not death; late love settles into us as spring romances never could.

Next day, unable to contain myself, I fling three protein bars, an apple and a copy of *The Rainbow* into my shoulder bag and head out to Kurama, the mountain that stands thirty minutes north of Kyoto by train, offering a long, steep walk through gates, up to a temple, along slopes said to be alive with spirits. Twenty-six years ago, on a November day like this, Hiroko and I walked up the mountain on a morning of mist and intermittent rain, drawn together but uncertain, since she seemed so rooted in Kyoto and I so constantly on the move.

The skies were a reflection of our hesitations when we set out, as I with my "birdlike" traveler's temperament, here for a year, shared adventures in Lhasa and Havana, and she got ready, at day's end, to return to her suburban marriage, the two small kids awaiting her. We looked around a turn and saw nothing but heavy clouds.

Today, the sun never falters. Excited matrons are gathering on the train platform for leaf viewing, their daughters having donned black stilettos to knock their boyfriends out. With each station, as the mountain train edges away from the city, there's a greater sense of light and space: rice paddies through the windows; hills, where there had been concrete apartment blocks ten minutes ago. At one point, the whole train passes under a gallery of trees, so full and close that their red and yellow hands seem to reach in through the windows to make us theirs.

It's transport into an illuminated text. At the tiny country station where I get out, young women in fishermen's caps are selling bean-paste rolls from a van, and along the village's single lane, everything is lit up, so you could believe diligent workers had been awake all night, polishing it to a sheen. I begin climbing the long slope towards the temple at the top, and then I stop for breath—this never happened twenty-six years ago—and pretend I'm halting for the view.

The other climbers, for the most part, are even older, if smaller, aided by sticks; they tramp past me without a word as if their entire lives were a climb and what awaits them at the top is nothing but the prospect of extinction. The only ones today who dawdle are two young lovers; they halt with every stride and play rock-paper-scissors to see who will climb the next three steps first. Separating and coming together again, playing with the notion of coming apart because they're so sure they never will.

I pass the bench where Hiroko and I once sat, and still the slope zigzags up and around, the old people striding past me. The air is chill up here, and a sign says, "1300 meters." But to what? More mossy slopes?

I stop for breath again and realize that, twenty-six years ago, we never made it to the top; we weren't looking at the temples or the leaves. When East Asian students are shown a painting, they notice the background as surely as their Western counterparts tend to see the figures in the foreground; perhaps I was leading Hiroko out of her home simply by drawing her attention away from the temple and flowering trees and neighborhood. In those days, I couldn't see that the best part of us is what's ordinary, nothing special.

Finally, I come to a slope that heads down—and down and down, for twenty slippery minutes through thick forest—and at the end I'm on a deserted country road, following a stream. Little red tables are set out beside a river, even placed on huge boulders above the water, protected by tall scarlet umbrellas. Women in kimono glide out from their restaurants, inviting me to enter the picture and become a sight myself.

I stop on a bench to eat my apple, accompanied by a can of sweet milk tea from a vending machine. Five college kids sashay past, on their way to climb the mountain from this other side—two boys and three girls. Odd numbers are a challenge, the ping-pong club has taught me.

The colors roar back in the intimate space of this postcard village along a sun-glinting stream; the trees are thick, and every lantern and red tablecloth is picked out. But it's 3:00 p.m. now, and soon the light will flare and begin to die; I realize, with a shock, that it was on this day, fifty-eight years ago, my parents got married. My mother has been eighteen years alone.

Five old people in their hats with their sticks, unstoppable, emerge around a corner and take the steps up to Kibune Shrine, the pretty little collection of wooden praying places that has been a famous appendix to Kyoto since the tenth century.

When I came here once with Hiroko, we began climbing those same steps, and then she turned back.

"You go alone," she said. This from the person who always loved being together, and in fact was regularly urging me towards shrines I had little interest in.

"It's more fun with two."

"I no want go."

"Come on."

"Please."

I walked up alone and inspected the typical cluster of shrines and doll's-house openings, the little shop selling protective charms against car crashes or bad luck in love, the wooden box into which the charms could be tossed, to be burned with the ending of the year. But when I asked her, after descending, if she was tired, she shook her head no.

"This shrine so dark! Everybody know."

It looked to me like any other place, offering protection and a place for meeting gods.

"You don't understand?" she asked, and made a strange kind of devil's face, with horns on either side of her head, saying something about placing candles above one's temples, since the resident goddess could turn herself into a demon.

"What are you saying?"

"Every night," she said. "This so famous! All people coming here, nobody can look." She goes on to say what sounds like something about blood sacrifices at the midnight hour.

"No!"

"Yes! Of course. Most important is nobody can see. Nobody watching. Many shrine this style. If want delay some person."

"Delete?"

"Delete some boyfriend or something like that." She grows quiet. "Spirit world so complicated."

Now the young girl on the walk has climbed three steps along. Now her beau has shown scissors to her papers and come up to join her.

Another golden morning, half asleep—I left my car in a parking lot in my dream, and now, for the life of me, I can't locate it—I feel the bed shake beneath us. The whole room seems to shudder for a few seconds, and then it steadies itself. Startled, I hold still, bracing myself for aftershocks. Each of our homes, on either side of the Pacific, is permanently girding itself for the earth to crack beneath it.

Sleepy, in pajamas that say "Happy Innocent Day," Hiroko murmurs, "My aunt little go brother house."

"You felt that earthquake?"

She shakes her head a bleary no.

"Your aunt went yesterday?"

"No. Twenty year before. Before lose mind."

Japanese has only two tenses, and in Hiroko's homemade, ideogrammatic English, things grow doubly conflated, especially as she's more comfortable in present tense than past, the way I am in French or Spanish. And Masahiro's spectral presence for twenty-three years only compounds the sense of losing track of where we are.

"She so clever. She find address, little go his house. But never knock door. Just want know he there."

"She loved your brother?"

"So close! He similar my mother. Anytime she looking him, my aunt thinking older sister."

But I remember, too, how Hiroko's brother, while their aunt was looking after them when their mother was in hospital, said, "Why should I listen to you? You aren't my mother." The poor woman broke into tears.

She'd always been Hiroko's protector; absolved from the competing interests of parenthood, but living round the corner, she'd taught Hiroko cooking and made her a special kimono for her twentieth-year coming-of-age ceremony. When Hiroko's parents briefly disowned their daughter, after she told them she was getting a divorce, it was her aunt who came running after her, along the line of ragged wooden shops, to assure her shadow daughter that she'd look after her, whatever happened. When we are old, she told Hiroko's parents, this is the one who's going to look after us.

But her aunt began to lose her memory in her seventies; and her marriage, as so many, had given her plenty of things she was happy to forget. Whenever she sees Hiroko, she lights up; the rest of the time, she smiles vaguely, staring straight ahead in the old persons' day-care center a few steps from where her older sister now lives.

"It's strange, don't you think?" I say. "All the time you were growing up, you were so worried about your parents. They were always in the hospital, your mother with asthma, your father with problems he'd brought back from the war. Every day, you were prepared to lose everything. And now your mother is eighty-six, and singing when we take her for a drive; your father barely fell ill in fifty years."

"True," she says. "That time, every day, I thinking, 'Maybe I never see mother again.' One time my mother and father little introduce circus. I so excited. Kinoshita Circus. All light gone. One woman in kimono walking on rope. Very sad, slow music."

"'Be careful,' say announcer. 'One mistake, she dies.'

"Such sad music, on and on"—Hiroko re-creates the downward-leaning tune—"and she walking such thin rope, in kimono, holding umbrella. I so scared, *monoganashii*."

The sadness of things; no one in Japan needed a reminder of that, especially in the years that followed war.

"After that time, I never want return circus."

"But here you are, fifty years on, and you have a grand-daughter, and you're well."

"Maybe," she says.

I see the spotlit figure on the tightrope, walking in the dark. Hiroko feels so innocent and without designs to me—women warm to her as much as men do—even though she's been through so much. Yet looking at our mothers, her aunt, is like seeing a preview of coming attractions; Hiroko is terrified—she keeps on trying to stem the habit while there's time—that I'll start hoarding things as my mother does, and I wonder whether she, like her father, will start abruptly cutting off friends. Or failing even to know who I am.

Last year, a young friend from Los Angeles came over for his first trip to Japan. His second day in the country, he asked if we could meet, and I suggested we get together in the musty and deliciously unswept Nara Hotel. We settled into two thick armchairs on an empty second-floor landing, and, very soon, he pulled a notebook from his bag and read me an observation about Japan.

It was a startling perception, the kind I could never have come upon after all my years here.

Then another, the kind that reasoning would never uncover.

"Where did you get all this?" I asked at last.

He looked at me to see if I was joking.

"No, seriously. I'd never see that in a million years. You must be blessed with exceptionally fresh eyes."

"You're kidding, right?" He looks at me and realizes I'm not. "You don't remember you wrote that in the book you brought out after your first year here?"

"Not at all," I say, genuinely taken aback. "I'd never be able to see that now."

Later, the same thing happens again. I marvel at the clueless kid I'd been, barely out of my twenties, wandering around Japan not knowing a thing and therefore seeing so much. It reminds me of the time last week when I had a revelation—change itself is an unchanging truth—so new and unlike anything I'd caught before that I had to scribble it down. A few days later, going through my notes, I found that I'd had precisely the same revelation, word for word, a year before. Eerily, on the same November day.

Later, I came upon exactly the same "discovery" once more, in my notes from six years before.

We're so convinced we're moving forwards, when all I seem to do is go round and round with the seasons, certainly no wiser, and often only more sure of how much I cannot know. Progress is a New World notion I'm not sure I believe in.

My neighbors dress up when they go to see the maples, as we might when we go to church. Old women look sleek and regal again in dark kimono, and the men beside them are sporting three-piece suits and trilbies as if posing for a turn-of-the-last-century photo. Girls from the countryside—and these days from Xi'an—pay two hundred dollars to get themselves up as geisha for the day, and the boys beside them, proud in indigo jackets and black Edo-period costume, present themselves as samurai protectors. "I can't believe we're seeing one!" cries a happy visitor from Minnesota as she snaps away at one such antique couple (and I take pains not to tell her that this is only a regular young woman eager to disappear into a geisha outfit for a day).

"Grandpa," calls back one woman as she stands with a fixed smile under a blaze of scarlet. "You got it?"

"Just a minute," fusses her husband while a gaggle of other sightseers clusters behind him to walk past.

I walk around Tofukuji, the great southern-Kyoto temple famous for its autumn colors, and the crowds are so intense that white-gloved policemen are standing at twenty-foot intervals, directing foot traffic to the left, and dozens of visitors are gathering on the temple's celebrated "Road to Heaven" bridge, under a board with a red line through a camera, posing for photos, while the guards shout, in English, "No photograph, no photograph!"

A very old man, leaning heavily on his cane, coat tightly buttoned, shuffles along a path beside an attractive young woman, fresh in her orange blouse—and a maple-haired beauty whispers "Date club" to her equally tall, lean beau as they pass.

I think of the time I was talking to a woman who'd lost her husband, a man who had not often been kind to her.

"If only he were here," she said, and started talking of all the happy times they could be having together.

"But you know he'd never change . . ." I began, and then I stopped, as I saw her face.

"Leave me with my illusions, can't you?" she all but spat, and I bit back my youthful foolishness. Even the illusions that wound perhaps preferable to none at all.

"Chee-zu," urges a woman with a camera, as she fiddles with the buttons and three friends stand with frozen smiles in front of her.

"No, no, don't worry," says the chunky old man with a gold tooth who is waiting to walk past to the next blazing corner. "We can wait."

The sun emerges from a brief disappearance behind clouds, and the whole grove of maples turns into a burning bush. I think of the old abbot of the temple—the place where Hiroko and I first met—who served so doughtily as Hiroko's protector for more than twenty-five years, offering to support her and her children when she got her divorce, encouraging her children to play hide-and-seek in his monastery (or get married there, if necessary), taking the three of them out for steak dinners. "Roshi," nine-year-old Takashi asked, "aren't monks meant to be vegetarians?" "Yes," said the Zen master, as his business card described him—a child of divorce himself—and cut into his filet mignon.

Whenever Hiroko called, he picked up on the first ring; when she asked if they could meet, he was always free, though in truth he was one of the busiest Zen elders in the land, in charge of 370 temples across Japan. Every time we walked down the private path to his monastery and Hiroko shouted,

"Excuse me," a responsive howl would sound from a junior monk within, and a shaven-headed figure in robes would appear to lead us down a series of narrow, polished corridors to the fourteenth-century audience room, where Fukushima-roshi, official Zen master, would emerge, a tiny, smiling figure in heavy orange silk robes, and take his place in a thick arm-chair. A young monk would be summoned to fetch us tea, and our friend would elucidate again the meaning of his calligraphy: "Every day is a good day."

One time, with a smile, Roshi announced, "I have five attachments." All of us knew that attachments are one of the main things Zen practice is meant to dissolve.

"First," he said, counting them out on his fingers, "Latte. Starbucks Caffè Latte. Then chocolate. Particularly Godiva. Third one, a little bit spiritual idea: bridge. In San Francisco, I always like the view of the bridge, a room with that view. The fourth is ice cream: Häagen-Dazs.

"Then, finally, fifth attachment"—he paused, and looked straight at us, with a confiding smile—"Joan Baez. I used to keep this one a secret, but secret is not good idea. Because students have many imaginings."

Though Roshi had seen his home destroyed by American bombs, and had felt obliged to become a monk at fourteen to protect the souls of his dead grandmother and sister, he was already drawn to the American spirit of openness, and soon he began touring the New World every year, explaining how Dirty Harry had Buddha nature and why his teacher told him to let go of any longing for understanding. In Zen practice, he explained, when you see a mountain, you should become that mountain. If you're observing the autumn, you become the autumn.

One time in America, he told us, after he'd confessed to his love of Häagen-Dazs, an impish student had asked, "How does a Zen master eat ice cream?"

"He becomes the ice cream," Fukushima had replied, delighting in his new name: "Roshi Ice Cream."

When we finished talking to him, the man who was proud to have been our "Cupid," the bridge in whose temple we met, rose out of his chair and stood beside it, small and round in thick robes, waving and waving with a broad smile as we walked across the large prayer hall next to his receiving room.

He stood there until we had turned a corner and were on a wooden corridor, shuffling towards the entrance.

But two autumns ago, when we went to see him, his hands were shaky as they reached for ours, fingers like thorns. He could barely stand, and he had to wave to us from inside his chair as we departed.

When he gripped Hiroko's hands between his own, to say goodbye, she shivered, and not just because of the chill. Six days after our only grandchild came into the world, Fukushima was gone, exiting the world on the day he'd been born, seventy-eight years before.

When I come back from my day of stolen radiance and step into our apartment, everything of Hiroko is there except the woman herself. The photos of our parents she's placed in indigo frames and set above the piano; the Vietnamese bamboo hat she brought back from Hanoi, her spare set of keys in the hallway. Her gossamer-light emerald scarf, draped around her black jacket from Milan. The small white tiger she's given me for protection, the gold Kashmiri stole and scarlet gown folded up not far from the tiny, bare blond wood desk at which I sit in one corner every morning.

The light, too, turning the panes of the window beside me into a color field of yellow and blue. In my twenties, watching the leaves scatter around Boston, I'd thought that autumn was the season that taught us how to die; only now do I see that in truth perhaps it's dispensing the much harder challenge of learning how to watch everyone you care for die. Death can be hardest on the living.

Then I tear open the envelope I've taken out of our clanking little gray mailbox downstairs. Inside, unexpectedly, I find a sheaf of thin sheets of paper, covered with small black characters inscribed in the classical style, vertically, to be taken in from right to left.

Who could be writing to us both, I think? And then I remember: the "Empress," as I always called her, with the beautiful tennis-honed forehand and the striking red headband, who welcomed us all with broad smiles every time the table-tennis club began.

One day, she arrived in the studio and never got up from her chair, clapping politely from where she sat. She didn't know what was happening, she told me; she felt dizzy. The next time, after a game began, she requested yellow balls, not white; her eyes were playing up. Then, one Sunday afternoon, I went to play in the local junior high school and found her, shockingly, in a wheelchair, blanket stretched across her lap. Then I never saw her again, and her husband, our deft and smiling leader, was gone as well. Off in a hospital, I heard, several train stops away.

On our travels, Hiroko and I managed to find a giant post-card of blue skies and a golden beach; I drafted a message, and Hiroko wrote it out for our friend in Japanese. Now I'm guessing we've received an answer; I lay the envelope on the table, for Hiroko to translate after dinner.

Right now there's a very blue sky. I can see through my hospital window a plane flying through the heavens. You move all across the world, Pico-san; such a nice life! As I watch the plane, I dream of looking everywhere in the world.

Last December I fell very ill. I lost all hope. I hit rock bottom. Slowly I began crawling up again. Everyone gave me love, and now my heart stands up again. I can't move, but I receive so much kindness. They teach me painting here, and poetry; I'm studying both. In the rehab center, I'm trying everything, very hard.

Today a nurse trainee is here with us for the first time. It's like a breath of fresh air.

I never forget you, Pico-san; your card is so beautiful! I look at it all the time—so lovely! I enjoyed ping-pong very much—such a beautiful memory. Thank you so much for your letter; I'm so happy. Thank you, thank you.

I must defeat this illness! Everybody is giving me love to help me knock it out. All my life I worked very hard at sports; I'm in bed now, but I dream that I'll feel better tomorrow.

Painting is very mysterious; I've cried so much, no more tears can come.

May your kindness give me power!

Next to the letter, our friend has enclosed five drawings: one of three bright-eyed puppies—"Looks like her," Hiroko points out, in a characteristic leap. A drawing of two kids waving from bicycles. Two paintings of snowcaps, a river beneath them. A still life of persimmons, harbingers of winter.

The next day, at the health club, I'm registering absences a little more. The seasons keep on circling around us, even as I seem to step into the same space again and again. People are moving back to their hometowns to care for elderly parents; others are receiving invitations from grown children to join them far away. This person disappears for six months—an eye operation—and when I meet Mr. Kyoto after I've been away and ask how he is, he says, "Very well indeed!"

But when he gives me a ride home, an hour later, he says,

"To be honest, I'm staying at home more now. A little while ago, I had to be taken in an ambulance to the hospital. And then again, a little later. A punctured lung: I had to have an operation."

I'm silenced.

"So I'm playing in the garden these days. I don't like to be completely idle. She"—he gestures towards his wife, sitting silently in the back seat—"doesn't like it. But I need to be doing something."

That book Mr. Joy gave me from the exhibition in 1974, I think now: he's probably moving to a nursing facility of some kind—he's so healthy, but who knows about his wife?—and doing his final edit on his life.

The third table in the studio today is taken over by two teenage boys, in flamboyant shirts, who are smashing the ball at each other, many feet behind the net, as if on a badminton court, and swinging wildly at easy lobs as if they've never played before. I watch my octogenarian friends dart across the space to hit pointed forehand winners from three feet behind the table, and think that seasons never go the way we think.

A wild ball clips the side of the table as it flies wide, and someone bows in apology.

"Lucky, lucky," says somebody else, in English, and I stop for a moment: where could they possibly have gotten that? I lose all sense now of whether that's a strange phrase I picked up from them, or whether the English-language mantra is something they picked up from me. Quite often these days, even the least friendly of the men, wispy hair flying as he spins the ball illegally with his hand when serving, says "Oh no!" when he nets it, partly in parody of me, perhaps, but also a tribute.

"Pico-san," says one of the matrons today, always too complimentary, "your arms are so long. Stand against Mrs. Nakajima for a moment."

I stand back-to-back with one of the older ladies, arms held out, and someone says, "Ten centimeters at least. No wonder you can hit so far to the left or the right."

Most of the men here are taller than I am, with far longer arms, but no matter. "Arms and legs so long," says a woman who's put on quite a bit of weight herself in the past year. "But stomach, well, it's a little . . ."

We go back to the table, and I, with a straight face, hit short spinless balls to Mr. Joy, knowing he'll swing for the fences every time and more often net an easy ball than a tricky one. I start aiming every shot to the backhand of Miss Tubby, as I think of her after her comment about my stomach, and she grows more and more flustered as she misses them, losing, more than the single point, her confidence. I've been here long enough by now to realize that not going for winners is the winning strategy.

Another woman then starts hitting hard balls fast to my backhand, and my replies fly off. *"Da-me!"* I cry, and smile: my involuntary curses are coming out in Japanese.

We change ends to begin a new game, and no one remembers quite whose turn it is to serve.

"It's Mother's turn," I say, "because she received after rock-paper-scissors last time." Hearing myself, I wonder who I am.

. . .

"Do you think it was going to the West that made your brother feel so far from all of you?" I ask.

Hiroko has come back from work and set a maple leaf she picked up along the road on our table; she's sweetened dinner with the latest news from the hip girl who calls her "rock-and-roll elder sister," the sixty-five-year-old with the clandestine lover, the one whose father won't allow her to marry her long-time love because he's from the outcast section of society.

"I don't know," she says.

"Do you think it was Jung? Or just that sense that therapy offers that there has to be an answer to everything, even a reso-lution?" If there's an arrow in your side, the Buddha famously said, you don't ask where it came from, or quibble about what kind of arrow it is; you simply pull it out.

"He always lone wolf," she says, though she could be talking about herself. "I more good mind-doctor than my brother!"

Perhaps; if only because she listens so well and then can relay one's forgotten thoughts back to one.

"He must be lonely."

She nods. "So sad. I pity my brother."

The days pulse on, rising and rising, it can feel, till the moment when they'll break. "Every day, I'm wiped out," a visiting friend from California tells me on the phone, "by a good-bye. People put so much feeling into it! I thought the Japanese would be poker-faced, restrained. But even the smallest moment carries such emotion."

"Maybe the end of the encounter is the time when people can best get out their feelings? Like us at a deathbed. In the middle of a meeting, it could be dangerous: You may say the wrong thing. Or the right thing may be taken wrong. It's only when it's all over—or about to be—that you can let everything out."

"Almost like the heart starts to open when the doors begin to close?"

"Well," I say, "it could be."

At the bus stop this morning, a freezing wind pushing my hands into my pockets, I look across the street to our second-floor window and see Hiroko, who's pulled the heavy panes back, waving brightly with both hands, back and forth, back and forth, as I board the 112 for the library.

"Pi-sama!" Sachi's bell-like voice chimes across the phone, the name she's given me and the way she says it a ringing blend of affection and singsong delight. Through most of our lives together, my stepkids and I have been quiet friends across the dinner table; they, being Japanese, are unwaveringly tolerant and polite with the strange, disheveled creature their mother has brought home—he might almost be an exotic pet who doesn't seem quite fatal—and their limited English and my limited Japanese has left us in a peace of smiling courtesies. But now that Sachi has returned from Spain with fluent English, I feel as if I've gained a daughter, as well as a wonderful confidante.

"How have you been?" she asks in her nation's tones of public cheer and warmth. After all these years, I never know—and Hiroko even less—what kind of sadness or worry Sachi might be pushing down. Hiroko, honorary foreigner— "My family little crazy Italian family," she explains to bewildered friends from abroad, "always so much emotion. I so sorry!"—broadcasts most of her feelings as clearly as the heavens.

"Are you enjoying your favorite season?" my daughter continues.

"I always do," I say. "As you know too well! It's hard to feel defeated in the autumn."

"What have you been doing?"

"The usual. Ping-pong. Taking walks in the temple gardens. Vacuuming."

She giggles. My disinclination to clean is a long-standing joke.

"Last night, I was watching an Ozu movie," I continue. "Do you know *Late Spring*?"

She doesn't, and I'm relieved. "I don't think you would like it."

Ozu's films are almost like panels in a single screen taking

us through the seasons, akin to the folded, lacquered paintings, human-high, with delicately traced branches on them, I
recently took Sachi to see in the National Museum. The characters bear the same names in film after film; we look in on
them as we might the neighbors we see every day along the
street. But whereas *Tokyo Story* now seems to be about Hiroko's parents, *Late Spring* is painfully close to the story of
our daughter.

A young woman is looking after her absentminded father,
a kind of professor and writer who, amiable enough, appears
unable even to make himself toast. She gets him tea and towels; she dances attention on his friends like a practiced hostess. She flashes an irradiating smile in every circumstance. It's
only when the father's sister points out that the girl is getting
old—so old that she might never get the chance to marry—
that the old man (my age, fifty-six) realizes that this cozy
arrangement, almost marital, is keeping her from the marriage
and independent life she deserves.

In classic Japanese fashion, the father gradually resolves to
pretend that he's going to get married so that his daughter will
feel free, even impelled, to pursue her own course. One form
of self-sacrifice tilts against another, and when his plot comes
to fruition, both characters savor its success by finding themselves profoundly alone, separated from the one person they
love.

The film becomes more and more crushing as it unfolds.
When father and daughter take a trip to Kyoto, they might for
all the world be a couple on a final weekend together before
separating for good. "We should have done this more often,"

the father says, as they begin packing their things. In Ozu, a wedding means the opposite of union—we never see the daughter's groom, a basketball player, throughout the film—and freedom means, in fact, the relinquishing of duties that can be life's deepest pleasure.

When the father, fragile on his cane, returns to an empty house at the end, assuring everyone that he won't be lonely, it's desolating. I'd looked up from the shot of his head falling down as he peels a summer pear, able at last—when alone—to admit his sadness, as the tide comes in outside, and thought how we've rejoiced to have Sachi back with us. She's stood by Hiroko's side through all the complication that follows a death, been capable when her mother was uncharacteristically lost, navigated the Internet to locate her missing uncle. She's set her hapless stepfather up with a printer and video delivery service, and with someone with whom to share his concerns about the family.

Yet, the more we relax into the blessing of her company, the more she's losing her life sitting by the phone, waiting for a call from Spain that never comes. As charming young boys circle around her, she talks pointedly about her "boyfriend" back in Europe, and Hiroko and I bite our tongues as the young men recede.

"So many time my father tell us," Hiroko says next morning, in the dark, "if family or parent, must choose family. Last year,

I say to him, 'Masahiro is a good son. He do what you say. Please, remember this. He listening your voice!'"

"What did he say?"

"Cannot say anything."

I imagine him fumbling, muttering darkly, as his own arguments are turned against him by his quick-witted daughter. "Who is the one who stood up to you when we were growing up?" she asked him recently. "You!" he chuckled. "You were the only one."

They're so much alike it hurts. He was always the one who said Hiroko's name most melodiously, even as she was shouting down the phone, at his failing ears, "It's Hiroko! HI-RO-KO!" And now that he's gone, Hiroko is him more than ever, and not only because she's de facto boss of the family.

I wonder anew how much Masahiro's impatience and violence might have come from his father. I was impressed—it served my interest—when Hiroko, walking out of her first marriage, said, "That life finish!" and barely looked back.

But now—fate's artful tricks at work—we're on the receiving end of the same brisk efficiency.

"My brother mind doctor," Hiroko says with early-morning impatience, "but he need mind doctor himself! Why he cannot understand my mother is old? She miss him."

"You said that he always thought you were your mother's favorite."

She nods. If he acts on that assumption, it will always be true.

"It's hard," I say. "Sons so often want to protect their mothers. Look at Takashi's friend." This classmate, who grew up around the corner—and often in our house—could never for-give his father for deserting the family in pursuit of a young woman.

Hiroko watches me warily; the central tug in so many a Japanese household is between wife and mother, and her first marriage died when she asked her husband directly, "Where are your loyalties? With your wife or your mother?" and he chose his mother.

"Is it pride, do you think?"

"Pride! Cannot change his heart. I don't know." She's often told me how her father and I have the same protective deity, according to the Japanese calendar. Fudo-myo, the god of fire. Sometimes known as the wisdom king who will not be moved.

I remember how her brother's father-in-law had shown up at Hiroko's father's funeral, to pay his respects; he, too, was bewildered, all apologies. He'd barely seen his two grand-daughters, though they lived a few train stops away.

"I never give up," she says now, and I tell her the story we all had to read in school, Shakespeare's *Winter's Tale;* the pass-ing of seasons sometimes brings us to the very positions we could never take before.

"Maybe it's different for women," I say. "Or wives." One day, the father of Takashi's friend, the one who had aban-doned his family, called up his ex-wife from Kobe, ninety minutes away. He was sick—close to death—and he had no one else to turn to. She called an ambulance, and hurried to the far-off hospital to be with him. The man died in his wife's arms, though his son was still in no mood ever to make peace with him.

. . .

Outside, the autumn is getting brighter, louder, if anything more resplendently bright. Like the signs eager merchants place on their front windows: "Closing Sale! Everything Must Go! Come Soon While It Lasts!" The opposite of the near-silent effects of the Ozu films I've been watching—the deliberate procession of steady still lifes—though, in the end, the feeling is not so different. Setsuko Hara, who takes on the name of Noriko in one Ozu film after another, smiles more brilliantly the more she's pushing down her losses; in life, as soon as Ozu died, the actress retreated to a house in Kamakura, where the never-married director was buried (under a black stone that says, simply, "nothingness"), and, unmarried herself, seldom showed her face in public again. It wasn't hard for the press to cast her as the true-life daughter she played in *Late Spring,* tending to her honorary father's memory till she became a nunlike figure in her nineties, coming out only to lay flowers on his grave.

I open the heavy glass door to our toddler's terrace—the washing machine gurgles and clunks, as ever—and I take out my tiny blue chair to sit in the jubilee light. *"Gambaranai!"* cries Hiroko from inside, getting herself ready for work. "You are a 'responsibility' person," she comes out and says. "Always want to try hard. Please, don't try hard today. Play, play, Pico!"

A bright cheerleader's dance ensues.

When I go to mail some letters three hours later, it's to find the makeshift farmers' market up again in the three-foot space in front of the post office: small boxes of onions and persimmons, sweet tangerines. A tiny old lady, fumbling with a string bag, shuffles into the place and asks my beloved protector behind the counter, "There are five of you here, right?"

"Five."

"Please," she says, and hands over a little bag containing five persimmons.

Down the street, in the park, six old men are sweeping leaves off a path, under the direction of an old woman wearing a black visor to avoid a tan. She looks uncannily like a riot-police officer with rifle raised towards demonstrators in the street. "Yes, over there, too," she barks. "And here. These leaves also."

Two grandmothers are on a bench across the green lawn, clucking over the colors. A very old man is leaning against a bench, doing push-ups. Across the street, a taxi has stopped, and a gray-haired woman steps out, very slowly. She gives a deep bow to the driver, to bid him depart, but, before she walks into her house, bends down to pick up two, three, four ginkgo leaves to carry inside.

I think of my friends in the West and despair of ever being able to convey the bounty of this life to them. They have their own equivalents, in every case, but the details of mine would make no sense to them, as if delivered in some version of Japlish.

Some of them have grown used to the same rhapsodies every year—my words and excitement barely alter—and simply assume that I'm drunk on the foreign substance of exoticism. Or lost in some paradise in my head. I cherish still the friend from high school—friends from England understand—who sent me a postcard after I'd left my Midtown office for a bare room in the middle of nowhere that said, "Sounds like you've gone mad. Well done."

"Don't you get bored?" the occasional new acquaintance asks, and I think about the light changing with every second at times, as new conditions appear and disappear with every week. Working four blocks from Times Square, where so much was so crazily in movement, I barely registered a thing.

"Don't you get lonely?" someone may ask, with kind intent, knowing how I've been stripped of my words, as of people who share my official interests. It feels to me as if I've walked out of a cluttered warehouse into a simple bare room with a scroll on the wall, everything so singular that emotion is brought to a pitch.

Of course, there's nowhere to hide here; in the absence of diversions, I'm alone with whatever haunts me. And every year the autumn poses the same question, which I, every year, am barely able to answer. There's no time to waste, the *yuzu*-colored light reminds me; and yet it would be a crime—a sin—to turn away from the beauty of the season. The bright days make me unable to resist the impulse to go outside; the days of sudden, unrelenting rain commit me to solitary confinement. I'm not always ready to accept that it's in surrendering my hopes and careful designs that real freedom comes—even though I have a wife who reminds me with every gesture that the only impulses to trust are the ones that arise without thought.

The lesson of the desk, really, though never an easy one to learn. I write and write, struggling to create this pattern and squeeze this point in, relishing the fact that this word or that—to no one but the author—turns in a hundred directions. And then I go for a walk, across to the ginkgoes and the old women standing under their light, marveling, and realize that I'm never in tune with anything unless I'm not in my solitary head at all.

The leaves have reached their climax now—cars are lined, bumper to bumper, along the narrow lanes of Kyoto, and uniformed guards stand outside the trains to push passengers into overcrowded carriages—as Hiroko and I hurry out to the bus stop at dawn and join the bankers stamping their feet in the early-morning cold, the nurses hurriedly applying mascara. At the local station, we take a train to Saidaiji, home to "the Great Western Temple" from the eighth century, and then another train to Takeda, near the eighth-century pagoda in southern Kyoto, and then another train to the conference-center hotel in a park in the far north of the old capital.

On the top floor of the hotel, a group of old friends of ours—seven men in suits, four red-robed monks—stands in formal silence outside a closed door.

It opens, and the Dalai Lama comes out. "Ah," he says—he gathers his gold-and-maroon robes around him with the help of an attendant—"an old friend," and comes forward to touch foreheads with me. Then he enfolds Hiroko in a bear hug.

"Little more weight, I think," he says, looking at me closely. "And less hair."

Then, tickling my chin, "But maybe more experience now!"

It's been our November rite for the last eight years, traveling across Japan with the Tibetans on their annual visit, almost the only outsiders to join the small circle of private secretaries, bodyguards and translators brought over from Dharamsala. I first met the Dalai Lama when I was a teenager, through my philosopher father, who had sought him out as soon as the Tibetan leader came into exile. Now, because I often write about Tibet, the Dalai Lama allows us to travel with him, and even to sit in on every one of his private audiences, with old friends, potentates, heavy-metal musicians eager for a blessing.

Sometimes we find ourselves stopping with his small convoy outside a deserted countryside 7-Eleven, where the Dalai Lama buys everyone a can of hot, sweet milk tea and stands at the entrance, extending a hand to bewildered truck drivers. Once we went with him to a crowded Yokohama shopping mall so he could buy some eyeglasses, and I watched him fondly rubbing the arm of the surprised elevator operator all the way up to the third floor. In an instant, we're out of our tiny neighborhood existence in Deer's Slope and whisked into a nine-story glassy Japanese parliamentary building, or a fancy lunch filled with the stars of fashion and society.

It's always a tonic and liberating experience insofar as the Dalai Lama is offering the world, in effect, a fresh pair of glasses. A change of perspective that is human, universal, not connected with any religion. When his longtime teacher died, he tells us this morning, he really felt sad. As if he'd lost his "ground," the foundation of his life. But then he realized that sadness was not going to do anyone any good. Better by far to try to bring to life the ideas his teacher had passed on, and to honor him in some more practical way.

His form of Buddhism couldn't be more different from the ones practiced in Japan; he's always urging—to little avail, perhaps—his Japanese audiences to forgo their chanting and backbreaking meditation for a more analytical grappling with the central texts of Buddhism, of the kind Tibetan masters, much more philosophical, enjoy. In truth, Tibetan monks probably perform more chants more ritually every day than their Japanese counterparts do, despite their official commitment to logic and science; besides, I've been in Japan long enough to see its freedom from abstraction and theories as its deepest liberation.

But what I get from his teachings, as someone who's too averse to distinctions to believe myself a Buddhist, is the sense of a knife cutting swiftly through projections to get to some sensible core. When someone comes to the Dalai Lama with a physical complaint and asks him to lay on healing hands, he says, "No, no. Much better to go and see a doctor!" When someone shares a grief with him, he looks at that person with an old friend's kindness and says, "Please, try to look at it from a wider perspective.

"If I have some problem in my life, or something like that," he goes on, "then, if I can see only that, it really looks impossible. Nothing I can do. You have to take a global perspective." All of us are intertwined, in his understanding, which means that everything is more subtle, less isolated than we think. So often what joins us all are the challenges that everyone must face.

This morning, amidst the long line of petitioners who file into his hotel room, we see some immaculately dressed Japanese dignitaries, with two Tibetan monks among them, who shuffle into his suite, four of them balancing a huge architectural model of a Buddhist center they're hoping to create.

The Dalai Lama greets them with warmth, welcoming them into his space and inviting them to sit down beside him. But he barely stops to look at the model, which must have taken large reserves of time and money to construct. "Instead of a Buddhist monastery," he says briskly, "maybe build a general learning center," from which everyone can benefit. And don't place it in some beautiful rural location, he goes on. Make it close to the city, so people can visit easily. A learning center "for the general science of mind," he concludes. "That would be of benefit for the whole world."

Being Japanese, the wealthy donors in suits and expensive silk dresses say nothing. But I sense this is not what they expected. In meeting the most visible Buddhist on the planet, they may have forgotten that his most recent book was called *Beyond Religion*, and stressed the universal values that lie beyond any one tradition.

As they start, hesitantly, explaining their vision of treasure rooms and meditation halls, he says, "No need, no need! This"—he warmly slaps the thigh of one of the monks beside him—"this is your treasure!" People so often get caught up in forms, he suggests, even though it's the core, the heart of the practice, that ultimately matters.

"I'm not much interested in architectural plans like this," he admits at last, having outlined his vision of a place of education devoted to the propagation of basic kindness and understanding, with nothing explicitly Tibetan or Buddhist involved. "It's like a toy, or something like that. When I was a child, I liked to play around with things like this. But those days are gone."

Then, as we take an elevator with him down to the lobby and walk out into the crowds gathered to take pictures of him, to seek blessings, to press books or white ceremonial scarves into his hand, I remember the last time Hiroko met him in Dharamsala. She'd fallen into the habit of going to spend every spring in a little guesthouse across from the Dalai Lama's home, sometimes waving to him as he was being driven out towards a meeting across the world, sometimes waiting at 5:00 a.m. to find a seat for one of his teachings.

One day, on her seventh spring there, he sent for her, and she met him between meetings.

"My parents are getting old," she said, "and I don't know what to do exactly."

"Spend time with them," he said. "Don't spend it here!" You're your own doctor, he might have been saying; you don't need to run out of the hospital to consult a doctor in a faraway land.

Many times when a wealthy petitioner asks him for a blessing, he says, "You are the only one who can give yourself a blessing. You have money, freedom, opportunity to do some good for someone else. Why ask me for what's in your hands?"

"Karma means action," he reminded Hiroko. "Not praying for blessings or good health, but working for them. You make your own karma every moment."

Now, as we head out into the sunshine—the northern hills of Kyoto are a blaze of russet, burnt umber, orange, under late-autumn skies of depthless blue—we're ushered into a back-stage room of sorts, before an afternoon conversation between the Dalai Lama and a celebrated novelist.

There are only four of us in the space: the Dalai Lama, Hiroko and myself, and a Californian monk from the Dalai Lama's temple who's also in our small traveling party.

"So," says the Tibetan, "what is the point of art? What is the larger purpose?"

Startled, I cite the Sixth Dalai Lama, famous for his poems and songs.

The Dalai Lama doesn't look very interested.

The monk mentions Milarepa, the mystic who composed poems in a cave.

The Dalai Lama looks dissatisfied.

In his way of thinking, looking closely at reality is the only thing that matters, not all the ways we make embroidered designs around it.

I recall the November day two years ago when all of us traveled up with him to a fishing village north of Tokyo laid waste by the tsunami of eight months earlier. A few miles out of the city of Sendai, we began passing along clean, modern roads lined by nothing but compacted trash, block-long rectangles of smashed cars and refuse. Telephone poles listed at forty-five-degree angles; a solitary chair sat in the open skeleton of what had once been a living room. Buses bobbed on the water beside us. When we pulled up at Ishinomaki—hundreds had gathered along the road there, behind ropes, to greet the famous visitor—it was to see nothing but a flattened landscape, which looked like pictures I'd seen of Hiroshima after the atom bomb. More than three thousand had lost their lives in this village alone, many of them children; nineteen thousand had lost their homes.

The Dalai Lama stepped out of his car and strode without hesitation to the people, mostly women, who had assembled in the street to see him. Many were sobbing, or calling out, in limited English, "Thank you, thank you." He held one person's head against his chest; he blessed another. He touched heads, shook hands, looked deep into one set of eyes, then another, asking, "What do you feel? . . . Are you still sad?"

"Please, be brave," he told them, as the women sobbed and others pushed forwards. "Please, change your hearts. You cannot change what has happened. Please help everyone else, help others become okay."

The crowd fell quiet; some of its members nodded.

"Too many people died," he went on. "If you worry, it cannot help them. Please, work hard. That is the best offering you can make to the ones you lost. Rebuild your community as your country rebuilt itself after the war."

It's the kind of advice that anyone might give, perhaps, but when he turned around, to walk towards the temple that had survived, gravestones in the foreground tilted crazily over or knocked down entirely, I saw the Dalai Lama take off his glasses and wipe away a tear himself.

Suffering is the central fact of life, from his Buddhist viewpoint; it's what we do with it that defines our lives.

Now, as he gathers his robes offstage, peering down to see how the theater's sound system works, I think of how, when we went into the temple in Ishinomaki, it was to see the bones of the lost, tidily gathered and placed in brightly colored boxes by the altar, under framed photographs, maybe fifty of them in all; in every case, Hiroko explained, there was no survivor to claim the remains, as Japanese custom decrees. "All lose parent," she told me of the five-year-old boys lined up cheerfully in uniform to shake the Dalai Lama's hand in the autumn sun.

After taking his place in front of the altar, the Dalai Lama began to speak, recalling the afternoon he had been told, at the age of twenty-three, that he had to leave his home, as well as his homeland, that very evening, if both of them were not to be destroyed. No time to say goodbye to his friends, no chance to take his small dog. Two days later, as he was crossing the Himalayas towards exile, a new life, he heard that many of his friends were dead.

At the end of today's session, we return with the Dalai Lama and his bodyguards and monks and secretaries to his hotel, hasten up in the elevator to the top floor and walk at high speed down the corridor with him to his room. His eyes are often red after a long day of events, but his pace never slackens. He's holding Hiroko's hand as he moves forwards; as in a physical expression of his teachings, he reflexively reaches for any set of hands to grasp between his own as he strides along.

Just before we arrive at his door, Hiroko says, "Your Holiness, we must leave you now. But thank you for everything."

He's on his way to Tokyo next day; we have obligations at home.

"Also," she says—her voice falters just a little—"I want to tell you: my father passed away this year."

Instantly the fast-stepping monk stops. He looks at her directly, deep into her eyes.

"When?"

"This year."

"What cause?"

"No cause. He was old. His body was tired."

He steps forwards and holds her for a long, long time.

Then he steps back and looks searchingly at her. "Remember: Only body gone. Spirit still there. Only cover gone."

He heads into his room and, at the threshold, turns around to wave at us briskly. "Good night, thank you." And then is gone as we head back into the golden flares of late afternoon.

All Japan might be holding its breath now, not settling to anything because a friend—the brightness of the warm days—is about to leave and there's no value in opening a new line of conversation or getting into anything serious. I walk through the suspended day, not quite autumn and not quite not, and follow the summons of the heart-clearing blue down to Susano Shrine.

The rice paddies are all plowed now; there's the smell of wood smoke everywhere. An old man is lighting a bonfire under the blaze of trees; an aged pal in rubber boots tramps up to him. Persimmons are orange balls against a rich blue sky, and as I take my leave of the shrine, I remember how Sachi and Takashi reported seeing flying squirrels in this area. Once, a sign reports, the whole forest was a network of shrines across the valley.

In our apartment, we turn the heater on, and feel too hot, headachy. We turn it off, and have to don thick sweaters. There's the sound of sniffles everywhere on the bus: people coughing, snuffling, one in every three wearing a white surgical mask, to protect us from germs, or to protect himself from us.

Last year, at this time . . . and I decide to kill the thought: Hiroko's father seemed the picture of health, only to be gone three days after he entered the hospital. Next year . . . I've given up trying to second-guess the world.

"You look happy today!" I tell one of my tall, ex-salaryman friends as he strides into the studio, earlier than usual, beaming broadly.

"I am," he announces. "I'm under the influence!"

The formality with which he announces his drunkenness is irresistible. He usually has a few beers, he's told me, after he's put in his exercise for the day, as reward.

"We had a meeting today of my old classmates," he explains. "In Kyoto."

"A reunion?"

"Kind of."

"How many of you came?"

"Twenty."

"Quite a lot."

"Well . . ." A Japanese way of saying "Not at all." Actually, he says, there were five hundred in each year in his day—fifty in each class—"because it was not so usual circumstances."

The war and the Occupation, in short.

"So you must have graduated in 19 . . ."

"Nineteen fifty-nine!" he says slowly, working it out in his head.

"But you were born in 1936."

"Exactly."

"You graduated from high school when you were twenty-three?"

"Oh, you're right," he says, laughing merrily. "I told you I was under the influence!"

"What were they serving at the lunch?"

"Chinese wine." He pauses. "And Japanese." An even longer pause. "And Western."

No kidding: this generally regal and self-possessed man smells today like a liquor cabinet. I remember the day the head of our circle, the Emperor, started running up and down the floor with a mop, and even more ferocity than usual. "Nakagawa-san is drunk!" a matron had exclaimed with delight. "He's had six glasses already."

Now, as we go to the table, my friend, uncharacteristically, lunges at a ball and misses. He flubs an easy shot, then throws a ball up for a serve and hits nothing but air. He collapses into embarrassed giggles, though not put out at all.

"You went all the way to Kyoto today, for a long, long lunch, and still you came back and showed up here at five p.m.?" I say.

"That's right!"

I remember the song-and-dance show I once saw in an elegant hotel in Nepal, in which the performers gamely kept flapping around at high speed, arms and silk robes flying, even as the lights went out across town and the music went dead.

The neighborhood is dark by the time I make my way back. The office ladies are tottering home on their heels through ghost-quiet streets. Some teenagers are heading out to after-school, shivering theatrically at the bus stop—the girls bundled up as if wearing coats three sizes too big for them—as I follow the trail of lanterns along the hushed, straight lines, between half-sleeping houses, home.

I look at my watch: Hiroko could be back twenty minutes from now, or sixty.

I used to kill the time while waiting for her by scrolling idly online or turning on the TV for a Japanese-language tour of Niigata that could put a hyperactive kid to sleep. But this night I decide to restore the time instead: I open up the man who first introduced me to the scripture of the autumn, Thoreau.

Thoreau, by his pond, reflecting on the seasons, might have been bringing into the New World the trees around Deer's Slope; it was he, after all, who was often said (mistakenly) to have introduced into English the essential Buddhist text, the Lotus Sutra, by translating it from the French. Sitting still was his way of losing himself in the world around him; "I suppose," he wrote, "that what in other men is religion is in me love of nature."

Driving up into the flaming hills of Concord in my early twenties, I'd made my way to his pond, eager to find out what the season meant (in England, November was just sludge on the ground, a steady drizzle, the unrelieved enclosing ceiling of low gray skies). I learned how for Thoreau it was a way of bringing people together, a "Commonwealth," the light on the commons being the rare kind of wealth to which everybody had access. "You can no longer tell," he wrote, "what in the dance is life and what is light."

But always in Thoreau there's the snag of something tougher, as of the branches of real life. He'd held his older brother, John, in his arms as John, only twenty-six, died of lockjaw after a minor cut. Eleven days after John's funeral, Thoreau had seen his beloved honorary godson and playmate, Emerson's five-year-old son, Waldo, expire after three days of scarlet fever. "Death is beautiful," Thoreau wrote, "when seen to be a law and not an accident." But every year, on the anniversary of John's death, he had bad dreams all night, and, till the end of his days, he had to leave the room whenever his late brother's name was mentioned.

The leaves "teach us how to die," Thoreau observed upon his deathbed, as he prepared the last lecture he ever gave, "Autumnal Tints," for publication in *The Atlantic Monthly.* Then added, with his characteristic drollness, "One wonders if the time will ever come when men . . . will lie down as gracefully and as ripe." Then he sent the magazine a scarlet leaf he'd carefully selected, for engraving as an illustration. His words quite literally outlived him, as the piece appeared five months after he'd been laid into the ground.

. . .

And then all reflective, woozy thoughts are batted into oblivion as Mayumi-san waddles into the studio again, for a cameo reappearance: a spherical Barbra Streisand on her final farewell tour.

The yarrow sticks decree—of course—that I'm to be her partner yet again, and she swirls her arms around in a way that could unnerve a team of Special Forces operatives. A shot flies off into the ether. *"Akan!"* she cries, local dialect for "No!"

"It's like this, right, Pico-san?" she says, trying to demonstrate what she was hoping to do. "Like this, no? What are you saying, Pico-san?" She bats me heartily on the elbow. "What do you know? I'm the expert here."

"No!!!" The cry is even more rending the second time. "It flew off. It flew off. Pico-san, what's happening? What the hell is going on?" Nearly all the points Mayumi wins come because the people on the far end of the table have dissolved into helpless bouts of laughter.

She's twirling herself around like an ursine ballerina the next time I try to cover rock with my paper, and when we win the equivalent of the coin toss, she throws her arms triumphantly up to the sky.

"We won, Pico-san. We won! The only thing we're going to win today!"

She never knows what the score is, so every moment comes to her as a shock. "What? Ten to two?" Then she collapses into abdomen-stretching, convulsive laughter it's hard not to catch like the flu. "As we get older," says an elderly gent in Ozu, "we seem to enjoy things more and more."

I wonder what dramas—even sadnesses—await Mayumi-san at home. I remember the elegant salaryman, silk scarf around his throat, who gave me a ride home once from a game and asked, "Pico-san, do you drink?"

"Not so much. I never developed the taste."

"I drink beer," he declares. "*Shochu.* And every night, before I go to sleep, I drink brandy."

He gives a deep laugh of satisfaction.

"You drink alone?"

"Yes. Sometimes with my son, when he comes home from work."

"Your wife doesn't drink?"

"My wife is sick," he says, straight out. "She got diagnosed with cancer two years ago."

We drive through the quiet country roads in silence.

Back in the club, though, with Mayumi-san, silence is forbidden. She rattles off some bulletin—or lecture, or imprecation—and when I see she's expecting an answer, I say, "Sorry, I can't quite follow."

"'Can't quite follow?' Pico-san, you don't understand a thing I'm saying? You haven't understood a word I've said? I could be asking for emergency help and you don't know! All this talking, and you can't follow a word!"

"It's such a waste."

"Isn't it, though?" And she giggles forgivingly. "Oh, I missed again. What? We've lost already?"

She collapses into laughter. Winning, losing, it doesn't matter; she's almost as unprofessional as I am.

As we're paired up again by the unbiddable yarrow sticks, I say, "I'm really happy. Mayumi-san is so terrible."

"What? 'Terrible?' You think I'm terrible?" And she's off and running again, thwacking me on the shoulder with her bat, not so gently. "'Terrible'? You're telling the truth at last!"

A part of me thinks, "Why do I always get my adjectives in Japanese reversed?" Another part thinks, "Why not?"

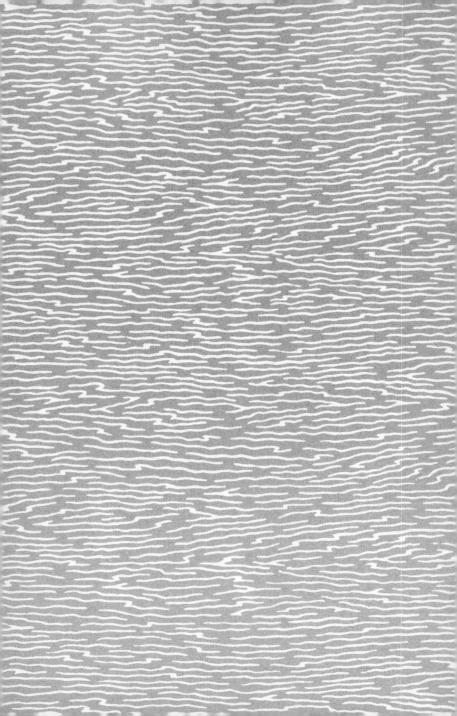

IV

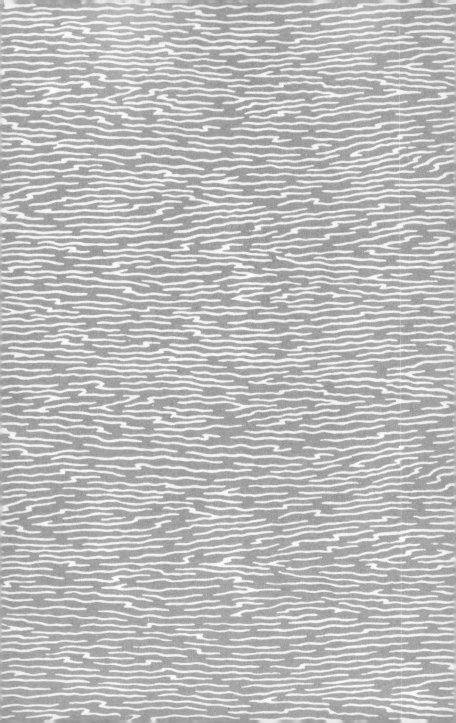

This road
No one on it
As autumn ends

—BASHO, near Kyoto, weeks before his death

Everything is burning now, though the days have lost little in clarity or warmth. The leaves are scraps of flame, the hills electric with color; as we fall into December, everything is ready to be reduced to ash. From the windows of the health club, I see bonfires sending smoke above the gas stations; I walk up through magic-hour streets and wonder how long these days of gold can last.

It still has the capacity to chill me: the memory of the flames tearing through the black hillsides all around as I drove down after forty-five minutes of watching our family home, some years ago, reduced to cinders. Death paying a house call; and then, when the house was rebuilt on its perilous ridge—where my mother sleeps right now—again and again, new fires rising all around it. One time after another, we receive the reverse-911 call telling us we have to leave right now, and we stuff a few valuables in the car, then watch, from downtown, as the sky above our home turns a coughy black, the sun pulsing like an electrified orange in the heavens.

"Everything must burn," wrote my secret companion Thomas Merton, as he walked around his silent monastery in the dark, on fire watch. "Everything must burn, my monks," the Buddha said in his "Fire Sermon"; life itself is a burning house, and soon that body you're holding will be bones, that face that so moves you a grinning skull. The main temple in Nara has burned and come back and burned and come back, three times over the centuries; the imperial compound, covering a sixth of all Kyoto, has had to be rebuilt fourteen times.

What do we have to hold on to? Only the certainty that nothing will go according to design; our hopes are newly built wooden houses, sturdy until someone drops a cigarette or match. As I climbed all the way up to our house, the day after everything in our lives was reduced to rubble, I saw that everything that could be replaced—furniture, clothes, books—was, by definition, worthless.

The only things that mattered were the things that were gone forever.

"Don't die before me," Hiroko says, holding me tight in the dark.

There's no sound from the street outside; only tiny white lanterns against the black.

"I'll try," I say, into her sweet-smelling, silky hair. "But I'm not sure it's something I have control over.

"So strange," I go on. "Your father was always so protective of your mother. You remember, when we were in California? All he wanted to do every night was to ask me to dial Japan, so he could report everything he'd seen to her. But she was probably really happy to be by herself, the first time in many years she'd had some days to herself."

"I never thought . . ."

"I know. Nor did I. He was the healthy one. Always so eager to run up the temple steps, even after he turned eighty. I never thought, too, that your mother would become so fond of him, in those final years. The more frail he—and she—became."

"He so happy that time. Little get prize."

Fifty-five years of steady companionship, and finally all sense of "what if" and preference falls away.

"Maybe it's better he went before her. He wouldn't have known what to do without her."

"Maybe."

The sun begins to show up behind the far-off hill, and the whole room becomes a box of lemon light.

When I step into the ping-pong studio, it's to step into laughter and movement. My friends are clustered round the seven playing cards laid out on one table, overturning aces and other number cards to choose partners. My old pal from my earliest days with the club, nine years before, is jutting her elbows back and forth, because she gets to play again. She's almost the only one who lets out a half-muffled cry of "I'm so happy!" when she wins a point or game; she gets so caught up in the competition that she seems not to have noticed how our un-official leader, Mrs. Kyoto, has given herself a losing card—she always does—so someone else gets a chance to have a go.

Always smiling and alert—she never speaks a word of English to me, after twenty-six years in the West; as Hiroko points out, she's a "harmony person," and doesn't want the others to feel left out—Mrs. Kyoto is now making sure that shy Mrs. Fukushima is ushered to the table, and that the one whose knee had been a bit dodgy doesn't feel she has to play just because her sitting out a game would mean odd numbers.

The one everyone calls "Doctor"—moon-faced, with his thick black spectacles and quiet, boyish giggle—is sporting yellow-and-black shoes with separate spaces for every toe, like gloves for the feet; six years after I met him, he suddenly declared, one afternoon, when we were the only two present, "It's rude, I know, I'm sorry, but could you tell me what you do for a living?" and offered, in turn, in English, that he came here from Korea, forty-six years ago. He, too, is eighty, I recall, as he spins around the table like a jack-in-the-box. I ask him about his son in London, and he says, "Hillary Clinton? Do you think . . . ?" and gives me a tentative smile.

"Kato-san, you look so healthy!"

"Always healthy," beams Mr. Joy, as I've dubbed him, in spotless whites. He still delights in talking about his trips to London, to Indonesia and Nigeria; when he was a boy, the only foreigners he'd see were soldiers.

"You're seventy-seven, right?" By this stage, his age is an achievement.

"Eighty," he says.

"But you never look tired."

"Five times a week, four hours a day," he beams, and then looks chagrined; his wife, I'm guessing, puts her foot down on those other days.

Meanwhile, I might almost be with my late father-in-law when I'm playing with Mr. Gold Tooth. The two of us have been rallying together for nine years now, he standing far back, hitting high, wildly topspinned lobs that I smash back, and often breaking into chortles as the exchanges go on. But he's the rare soul here who doesn't seem to know how to read the air, as they say in Japan. He deliberately hits balls that will throw out some of the less graceful older women; the point is won, but the trust of everyone else is in a second lost.

And who knows what he's leaving at home? He's here every morning at 9:30, to do aerobics, in Hiroko's class; he's still playing ping-pong at 6:00 p.m., when I leave. We've heard about a wife, but we never see her; every time I spy his small figure walking alone through the streets at dusk, I wonder what awaits him.

The Empress is still in hospital; we see her husband, smiling brightly and murmuring apologies as he clings to a strap in the crowded bus. The man with the unruly white hair and the pretty young wife—a professor, I assumed—disappeared overnight (cancer, it was whispered), and then his wife was gone, too, back to her first home, in the countryside.

· · ·

Yet, every time I come back from a trip, everything seems much the same. I'm carrying the call to prayer above the flickering lights of Jerusalem inside me, or the intricate alleyways around the blue-tiled mosques of Isfahan, and my friends are exchanging fast forehands, squealing over long rallies, looking a bit askance if a new pair of matrons appears and takes over our third table.

None of us ever gets any better: Mr. Joy is still whamming his smashes from six feet back into the net; the matron with the girlish demeanor is still swinging wildly at any ball with backspin and failing to make contact. Skills occasionally improve, but only as joints and limbs begin to decline, so we're all joyfully back where we began. The seasons turn and turn, and we seem to go nowhere at all.

Looked at up close, of course, the group is constantly shifting. There have probably never been two days when exactly the same combination of people has shown up. But that's the beauty of a group, a larger piece of music; the river's always the same, as they say round here, even though the water's constantly in motion.

I walk in, next day, to find the whole group clustered around Mr. Gold Tooth; I go over and see that he's excavated some photos from when our circle was formed, almost a decade ago.

"Look at how young you look!" "Look—you're just the same." We see a photo of the Empress, and no one says a thing. Finally, one woman offers, "Such a shame!"

Empowered by the impromptu viewing, a shy older man with neatly combed white hair—his quiet manner gives no indication of his killer forehand and backhand slam—brings out his phone, and shows us a picture of the maples. He and his wife, he explains, to universal acclaim, drove an hour or more to the place where the leaves are famous for lasting longest, and have brought back some mementos for us.

He might be a teenager on a first date, I think—so ready to find excitement from the same seasonal blaze he must have witnessed more than seventy times by now. Why, I wonder, must I so often be running against time, when I know that the only way to be happy is to make my peace with the autumn, and see it as a friend?

"You remember when you called Roshi after Sachi went into hospital?" I ask Hiroko after I get home; I must be thinking about how foolish it is to protest against the seasons. The lanterned narrow streets of our modern Western suburb look like a nineteenth-century woodcut in the dark.

"Cannot forget," she says. "Your idea!"

It was indeed. I didn't know where she could turn when our daughter received her chilling diagnosis, so I suggested she call her constant friend and guardian, the Zen master.

"So terrible idea," she says as she lays down the salads she's brought home for dinner. "I never forget. That time little working Gere clothes shop, next station. Lunch break, I have time, I call."

Her daughter was in hospital, with Hodgkin's disease, she told the kind older man, who'd never said a word of admonition to her when she got her divorce, and offered to protect her in every financial or legal way that mattered.

"Everyone dies," he said sternly. "That's the law of existence. Every life concludes in death."

"I so shock," she says now. "I hoping he say some kind word, give me power. But opposite!"

"He's a Buddhist. That's his job: reminding people of impermanence. Carrying a sign that says 'Nothing lasts. Nothing is as good or as bad as it seems.'"

"I know," she says hotly. "All I know! But that time, I so upset. Little door closing in my life."

We hear a mother calling to her son outside, and then a high voice calling back. "Later, I wake up. Little *keisaku*." The wooden stick with which Zen students hit those nodding off in the meditation hall. "I cannot ask other person. Must be strong myself. Other person cannot help.

"Now I so happy thinking that moment. But first time I hear, so sad."

Winter is the time when my new friend Gerold, an oncologist from Germany, comes to visit, and we take a walk together around Nara's deer park. He, too, had felt an uncanny sense of recognition when he began to explore Japan—here was the home that had been waiting for him forever, it seemed—and he'd written to me, a stranger, after reading my old book. Now, shivering at the bus stop, I look down the long, silent avenue of bare-branch ginkgoes—the tree like the one under which the Buddha had his moment of clarity; the rare living thing to survive the bomb on Hiroshima—and head off to meet my friend beside the statue of the monk in central Nara. In the bright, chill afternoon, we take a long stroll through the line of stone lanterns to what is sometimes called the holiest Shinto shrine in Japan, outside of Ise.

"That drug I told you about," says Gerold, as we note how the cherries are the first to lose their leaves, "the one I've been working on for years. It's coming up for FDA approval, finally."

"You must be excited."

"Yes," he says, "and no. Even if it is approved, it will give a patient only a median of three months, or maybe less, of extra life. It really makes you think." The deers' cheeks are getting puffy in the cold as we reach the "floating" pavilion that sits on a pond surrounded by hills. The does are growing heavy, the mating season behind them.

"Because, of course, it's not how many days you have that matters. Only what you do with them."

A young couple is sauntering between the trees. We pass the old wooden house used for storing Buddhist texts, a grove of wild plums. The papers, I say, are full of stories of what happens when people live and live, and autumn lasts till February. An eighty-two-year-old man slips too many pills into his wife's tea because he cannot bear to see her suffer. A seventy-six-year-old is found collecting the pension of his father long after the older man has died. A third of all suicides now are over sixty-five.

"Actually," says Gerold, as we count the cost of this inner climate change, "the miracle is that so little goes wrong. If you look at the hundreds of billions of cells in the human body—one hundred billion in the brain alone—and if you think that any one of these could go wrong, it's quite amazing that we stay healthy so long."

Branches are witchlike as I walk across the Deer's Slope park. The path is still carpeted in scarlet and orange, so thick I might be walking on a crackling, seething Persian rug. The light remains sharp, exuberant, and the evergreens look robust, but, with no leaves to filter them, the rays have nothing to alight upon but a barren landscape of gray and black and blue.

One woman is running up and down in place between the trees, on red and reddening leaves. Another holds a brown bag against her face, to protect it from December sun. "Look, Grandpa," cries a young woman—caregiver or granddaughter?—to a man hobbling past on a cane, as ghost leaves shiver down from the bare-branch maples.

When I head onto our little line of shops, it's to find a Christmas tree on the sidewalk, outside the Père de Noël patisserie; inside, the perpetually fresh-faced, ponytailed wife of the pastry chef has placed Christmas caps even on the two white chairs set out for customers in line. A bear is sporting a floppy

Santa hat above the éclairs, while a soft-voiced Japanese girl on the sound system delivers a plangent Japanese rendition of "Silent Night." The honorary anthem of Deer's Slope.

By mid-afternoon, when the dying light is turning homes to gold, I see the Seven Dwarves on one lawn, not far from the flamboyant house where Mickey and Minnie stand. When first I arrived, I couldn't get enough of such absurdities: of course Happy and Bashful were ubiquitous here, I decided, in this land of small, diligent souls who whistled while they worked and formed a tireless team to protect the foreign-seeming white princess at their heart.

But irony has nothing to bounce against in Japan, and ends up like a pun in a foreign language. Objects are only as important as the emotions they awaken. If Sneezy and Dopey and Doc can give rise to the same earnest fascination as the Three Wise Men, why quibble over details? The celebrated images of Santa on the cross that foreigners laugh at in this season are simply ways in which Japan takes everything it wants from everywhere, and makes it cute, or a source for fresh emotion. In California, Hiroko loves everything about the Zen temple I introduce her to except the fact that the angriest person there is sporting a T-shirt bearing the Japanese character for "love."

"I really don't trust myself," I say to Hiroko after I come back from the post office. They've set out blankets beside the little ATM kiosk at its entrance, even though the place is protected by two doors and admits no wind. The stacks of New Year's cards for the coming Year of the Horse are almost down to nothing.

She stiffens at the table.

"No, I don't mean like that. I just mean that I can't trust a single perception. That sentence that seemed so vibrant yesterday, it's flat and dead today. That street that was a flood of gold this afternoon may well be no-colored gray and puddling rain tomorrow. You're always scratchy and tired at four-thirty, the way I stop making sense at eight p.m. Night thoughts invariably seem unbalanced in the morning. How can we find importance in any of our responses?"

"You writing this in your book?"

"It makes all writing irrelevant."

In parts of Kyoto, as we take the long series of trains into the city twenty miles away next morning, the hills are still a blaze of color, though a skirruping wind is turning the leaves into a snowstorm, a shower of the kind we see with the lighter blossoms of April, but brilliantly colored now instead of white. When we get to the little building just around the corner from the glassy, futuristic Buddhist university, a young woman greets us at the entrance and hands us white masks to place around our mouths. In winter, you can never be too careful.

Then she presses the code in the elevator and we're getting

off at the second floor. Hiroko's mother is in the small common area as we approach, and waves at us gamely, vaguely, with both arms, as if sending out an SOS.

"She doesn't know who we are," murmurs Hiroko, under her breath.

"Sumiko-san," says one of the ever-patient nurses, bustling over to the old lady. "Look who's come! Your daughter. Let's get you into your room so you can talk to her. Aren't you lucky to have a daughter who lives so close?"

We head into her tiny cell, the two large orange Beanie Baby cats Hiroko brought back from California sprawled across the bed, a line of pink silhouette teddy bears on the wall. Printed sheets, a futon decorated with whales and dolphins, a pink-and-white striped pillow. The furniture of early spring.

From the dresser, her late husband beams down—a little wan in his later years, but glowing as he dandles his great-granddaughter.

"Where's Grandpa?" the old lady asks. "Is he in Hiroshima?"

"Yes," says Hiroko, resolving to try a new tack. "He decided to see his sister. You're not jealous, are you?"

"Oh no," says her mother. "Why should I be jealous? He's with his sister."

There's a knock on the door, very soft, and a caregiver comes in with three tiny cups of green tea and some cakes wrapped in cellophane. I pull out the chocolate cake and doughnut I've bought for my mother-in-law.

"Oh, thank you." She smiles at me, the tears of our first meeting long forgotten. "So tasty!"

Then she looks around her.

"Masahiro? Did he die?"

"No, Mother," says Hiroko. "He's fine. He thinks of you all the time."

"Is that so? He didn't die."

"No, Grandma!"

"I haven't seen him for a long time."

She munches happily on her cake—"So tasty!" In the past, this tiny woman never had much of an appetite.

"And Grandpa, he's in Siberia?"

"That's right."

What is the self, I think again, if so quickly it turns into something it couldn't recognize two days ago? I remember the time my friend Michael, a longtime student of Zen, told me how sometimes, in delivering a sentence, he omitted a "not," reversing the meaning entirely. "But nobody seemed to care," he said. "Oftentimes, we're responding to a tone of voice, a feeling. The words aren't so important. Especially in Japan."

I told this story to a Buddhist-minded friend in California, and she said, "How cynical!" But to me it sounded the opposite: an expression of faith, in something deeper than mere words. Words have little value in the kingdom of essential things. They're just decorations on the feelings too deep for us to put into syllables.

"He's sending you love letters, Grandma," Hiroko says, because it's true: she discovered, while cleaning out the wooden house, a whole cache of letters her father had sent, and held on to for sixty years. "Love letters from Siberia."

"He is." Question or statement, it's hard to tell.

"He loves you so much."

Just one change of a letter, and a death is reversed. The old woman shows off to me the two toy cats who, for all the world, might be the living kittens she's always loved, though more amenable.

Eager to divert her, Hiroko pulls out her phone and shows her mother pictures of the old lady's grandson, her great-granddaughter.

"Masahiro," she says proudly.

"No, Grandma. That's Takashi. My son, your grandson."

"*Ah, so.* This one is a woman, no?"

"No, Grandma! That's your grandson. It's just the hat that . . ."

"I'm sorry," the old lady says, smiling over at me. "My mind's broken."

She doesn't seem perturbed. "My mind's totally broken," she says, and chuckles happily.

"I was such a pretty little girl. So beautiful. Everybody used to ask my mother, 'Where did you get such an adorable daughter?'"

There's a pause as she eats.

"My mind's broken," she announces.

When we walk out into the sun, Hiroko's a little rattled, as I would be. Sometimes her mother asks, "Why? Why? Why?" as a child might. But a child is coming into understanding, and this one is leaving it behind. "I think it's best to stick with ani-mals," I say. "And candies." I know: I show my mother pic-tures of her beloved cat and she breaks into delighted smiles every time, becoming again the person she was when the cat was snuggled next to her in the chair.

At one point, when Hiroko pulled out an old photo album and showed her mother some black-and-white snapshots of a trip in a boat in the 1960s, the old lady said, "Who's that?"

"It's you, Grandma!"

"Me?" She looks closer. "I see. It's me."

"It's you, Grandma. Don't you remember?"

Around us, the ancient capital, with its sixteen hundred Buddhist temples and four hundred Shinto shrines, is a rash of red, white-bearded Santas. At the huge central post office, the "Official Santa Mail for Finland" box is still on display, though most will have sent their greetings long since, as Takashi did when young. In Tokyo, there are said to be two hundred per-formances of Beethoven's Ninth Symphony in the Christmas season alone, as people flock into churches to hear of Jesus's birth and to sing "Adeste, Fideles."

Just a kind of air freshener, perhaps, a mood sweetener, to keep public cheer at its regular level. Anyone who's fallen in love because she longs to forget where she is—or who—knows how that works.

Maybe Masahiro will never make himself visible again, I think, but all of that comes to seem immaterial in so many ways. His mother sees him, everywhere she looks. "He came to visit me last night," she told Hiroko a week ago.

"He just wanted to make sure that I'm okay." She can protect the side she loves of him, and let the rest fall away. Even if that's part of the impulse that drove him away in the first place.

So much of the fretting—did I put a "not" in that sentence? is he thinking of me now, and if so what form does that thinking take?—just a kind of idle, useless scratching of the mind. Because then the weather changes, and the next morning, the house has burned down, and all those worries are wiped out along with it.

"Everything Is Nothing, Nothing Is Everything" was one of the sentences that our Zen friend in Tofukuji used to scrawl across huge sheets of paper in his unhesitating black calligraphy; we can see the gray roofs of his temple floating above the two-story buildings in the neighborhood, like a ship waiting to carry us off across the seas, when we take the train from the nursing home into central Kyoto. It was him in six words, really, and his tradition: an easy paradox if you look at it one way, but something much more haunting if you've seen everything you care for dissolve into smoke and dust, and then realized that that smoke and dust are everything.

When we stop off at Hiroko's parents' home later in the day—everyone is preparing the little lane for New Year's, when two and a half million people will throng, almost impassably, up the two blocks to the shrine—the past comes flooding back as Hiroko lights the incense on her altar, guarded by the framed photos of her father and her grandmother.

"Every year, we little play Monopoly," she says. "New Year time, so busy. Crazy busy! So many people coming shrine. You cannot imagine! All night, cigarette shop open. We cannot sleep.

"Then, three day later, so quiet. All Japan sleep. We sit under *kotatsu*"—the heated blanket placed under a low table that suggests a hearth—"and play game."

"Who won?"

"My brother. Every time. So clever. He such good plan. Make hotel—Pennsylvania Avenue, Park Place. I must pay more, more money. Soon all money gone!"

"Better than going to jail," I say. And maybe not so different from where we are now: going round and round, passing Go in order to move round again, rolling the dice, paying rent. The Game of Autumn.

At the top of the narrow, creaking set of wooden stairs, in the two rooms so small they might be prison cells, she starts bustling through a chest of drawers.

"Look," she says.

It's the poems she discovered earlier in the year, after her father's death. Neatly typed out into a kind of laminated poster by Sachi.

"My father so romantic! I never expect. Always he little thinking hometown."

She hands over the poems.

Please come and see Hiroshima.
Before, dead bodies everywhere.
Now, a beautiful new town arises.

And, underneath,

When young, so many dreams.
Now—nothing but soap bubbles.

Dead bodies everywhere in the poems: the ones he witnessed during four years in Manchuria, three years in Siberia,
the ones that awaited him on his return to Hiroshima. Every
other street in Kyoto has a trim wooden board announcing
the people who were slaughtered there, or died in some coup
d'état.

"Maybe your brother will forgive his father one day," I say,
as we see what we could almost never see in life: what was
inside her quick-tempered, stoical father.

"You, too," she says, and I start.

Back home, Hiroko, like all the neighbors, is busy again, polishing Buddhas, sweeping up salt, preparing to pound rice for
the special treats of New Year, one of the other times when the
departed return, but accompanied on this occasion by neighbors and old friends. Everyone is punctilious about observing

the first sunrise of the year, the first meal, the first visit to a parent; after the stained-glass radiance of last November, winter brings blue invigoration and the promise of a fresh start.

I, meanwhile, start gathering my things to return to California; my mother, grateful child of British India, celebrates Christmas with the vigor of a Hindu-born Theosophist who grew up surrounded by Christmas trees, Advent calendars, Christmas puddings, Wesley hymns. Even in her eighties, she drives to the supermarket to buy a live tree, around which to open presents on Christmas morning; until very recently, she'd steal down in the dead of night on Christmas Eve to leave a stocking outside my bedroom, full of Trader Joe's treats and gift cards for books.

A way to keep her only child a child, perhaps, consoling; but no bad thing, I've learned in Japan, if it gives her a sense of youthfulness and long futures. The symbols mean everything if you accept the feelings that they carry.

When I wake up, after midnight, I look in on Hiroko and see her enfolded in her thick futon in her room, her heating blanket underneath her, uncharacteristically motionless; she has the gift of making everywhere she inhabits a warm, cozy nook, even as her strange husband reels through the night in fractured dreams of missed flights and foreign hotel rooms.

It feels odd to turn the tables: so often, even now, I'll sense something in my sleep, somewhere between full consciousness and dreams, and open bleary eyes to see her standing in the dark, looking down at me. Just as she did, twenty-six years ago, when we first met.

At the ping-pong club, the smell of liquor is stronger now. Everyone's heading off, every other day, to year-end parties; they all might be back in a children's calendar of classmates' birthday parties, like the one where I first visited Hiroko. A rich, chatty lady with long dark hair—well over sixty-five, I'm guessing—says, "Pico-san, please teach me," which is the polite Japanese way of saying, "Let's have a game!" and asks me to show her how to hit a backhand slice on return of serve.

We hit a few practice shots, and then some backhand drives, and another woman, small and voluble, says, "Wow, Pico-san: so beautiful!" My backhand topspin is just the shot I never trust and about which I've always been embarrassed.

After all these years as a tourist here, observing, I seem to have one small thing to offer.

"Like this?" asks the small woman, flipping her backhand with her wrist.

"Yes, yes. Exactly!"

As I walk home, I look at the sturdy-seeming houses and shiver for a world of wood and paper. Fires are such a constant visitor in Japan that there are separate words for a fire caused by accident, a fire caught from the next-door house, a fire set off by an incendiary device, the condolence call after a fire. In Tokyo, it used to be said, a house was built for only three years, so likely was it that fire would visit soon.

The buildings are much less fragile now, but out of one I can hear the mournful chorus of "Auld Lang Syne," here a song renamed "In the Gleam of Fireflies" and ending with the pregnant lines:

Light of fireflies, snow by the window
Suns and moons spent with books.
Years have gone by without a trace.
It's daylight now, and we must part.

When Hiroko and I first met, much of our talk was of endings. Of course: I had come to Japan for a year, and Hiroko could see I was the kind of fool who stuck to my plans, even if circumstances suggested I should work with a larger logic rather than against it. She, meanwhile, was in the process of tearing up the life she'd made and burning down her house: preparing to leave her husband, take off on her own with her kids and commit herself to everything that was unknown to her, stepping a little away from the collective script that is Japan's unchanging musical score.

I, by contrast, came from the world of Hollywood endings—the clinching kiss over the final credits, the tidy resolution of every plot point, the kind of therapy-inflected "arc" in which her brother perhaps believed, now that he was studying Jung in Zürich. In the New World, unlike in Japan, baseball games never end in a tie.

And I, no less, was recalling through the fog what her culture was slowly beginning to show me, in those Ozu movies named after spring or autumn: the seasons cycling round so you can see the folly of trying to put a human period on a rushing stream.

The yin-yang earrings that she wore the first time I visited her house were the first thing I noticed: no black-and-white in Japan, since every end marks a fresh beginning, and in every forgetful love, there's an urgency born of the sense that nothing lasts forever.

"You remember the story Fukushima-roshi told us the final time we saw him?"

She remembers.

Our Zen master friend had found himself in New York City, on one of his final tours to teach Zen practice across the New World, and he'd heard that his near-secret fifth attachment, Joan Baez, was appearing at Town Hall.

The concert was sold out, but he sent some of his monastic attendants out onto Forty-third Street to scalp some tickets. Pulling wads of cash out of their robes, they'd managed to score four seats, quite close to the stage, in the very center.

That night, when the singer, close to seventy, delivered her rich soprano renditions of "Where Have All the Flowers

Gone?" and "Forever Young," it was to see three Japanese monks in full black robes flapping up and down in front of her, dizzy with delight and relief. At their center was a small, shaven-headed figure in thick golden robes, visibly transported, not long before Parkinson's rendered his smallest move impossible.

"Though the years are sad," I read this morning on our terrace in the sun, on the last page of Edith Wharton's autobiography, "the days have a way of being jubilant."

I know I could track down Masahiro if I wanted—but what could I tell him that he doesn't know already? I see him in his closet, as when he was a boy, calling out, "Please, let me out! Please! It's dark and lonely; I'm scared." But the only one who can let him out now is himself, and interference from outside could easily throw off such a delicate instrument.

As Hiroko stirs in the predawn dark, I hear her say, as if half in dream, "That time, my father so, so tired."

"What time?"

"Last time I go with him to shrine.

"He say, 'I want die!' He never say like that before. I tell him, 'You cannot choose. Only God can decide. You must be strong!'"

"He was worn out from looking after your mother."

She nods. Only one week later, his body did give out, and he was gone.

"All night," she continues, "I singing song for my father. In hospital." She's never told me this before. "His favorite."

About the sun going down and his friends being laid in the ground, as he thinks of his beloved Hiroshima.

"I singing time," she says, "he so, so calm. Never close die. Then nurse little introduce me bed. I sleeping, two, three hour. When I wake up, he gone."

"He's lucky. No pain, no struggle. You beside him."

"I know. That time I promise . . ."

And the sentence trails off.

I walk out before the light comes up, as Hiroko falls into sleep again; I need to imprint this scene upon my mind to sustain myself through the weeks to come. The kindergartners scattering across the lawn, in pink and blue and yellow hats; the old man shuffling along the path to catch the last maples in his viewfinder. The grandmothers padding around in pink slippers, as if the entire neighborhood is their home.

As I come back down onto School-dori, I notice that a heavy mist has gathered while I've been waiting, so that now I can scarcely see the post office fifteen feet from our home.

When I step into the flat, Hiroko is bustling around at high speed, flinging open doors and windows, preparing to carry the futons out.

"You don't know?" she calls out as I saunter in. "Mist mean sun is coming soon!"

. . .

A week from now, the days will start to grow longer again, and cycle towards spring; sprigs of plum blossoms will appear in a tall jar in the entrance hall to the post office, and people will be on alert to see the bare branches begin to put on their floral dresses again. On the solstice, the dead are said to be within reach once more; Hiroko will take her family newspaper to share with her long-departed grandmother.

All thoughts of what is home and what is not dissolve as I arrive in the park on an unseasonably warm afternoon. The little girls running, screaming, up the ramps to the Spanish galleon might be my neighbors, and the fathers kicking soccer balls to sons could well be my ping-pong buddies' kids. As I step into the damp old gym, Mr. Joy offers me a wave from one corner, and a matron presses a doughnut on me ("For later," she urges, when I say I've just eaten).

No sign of my flirty, lipsticked friend. The last time I'd seen her, five weeks ago, I'd asked, reflexively, if she was well, and she'd said, "No," and given me such a long medical answer that I feared the worst.

When I say that I'm happy to be here since I'll be gone again soon, a gaggle of women gathers round me to ask where I'm going. "California? Waaah! Hawaii? So cool!" But the going seems less important now than the coming back; the autumn waits to greet me, many returns from now.

. . .

"What kind story your book?" Hiroko asks, just two mornings later; a no-color blur is coming through the windows, and when we notice how all shade is absent, we pull back the doors and see snow drifting down, burying the already silent lanes of the quiet, rectilinear neighborhood, making everything new.

"You writing autumn story?"

The fact that she has as little a sense of what I do for a living as I do of what she does has always been a shared relief; one fewer area to muddy with second-guessing.

"Not so much story," I say. If autumn is a religion, it's something you recite—or see with your eyes closed—more than put into words.

"Like Ozu movie?" she asks in apprehension. My attempts to inflict the seasonal explorations of mood and dissolving families on her have not been a success; when I watched *Late Autumn*, the same film as *Late Spring* essentially, but with Setsuko Hara playing the mother now instead of the daughter, the one losing a child rather than moving away from a parent, I spared Hiroko and watched it alone.

"You know me," I say. "I'm so greedy for sunlight, I need to be pushed into the dark."

"Your book, nothing happening?"

"Well, not exactly nothing. But what happens is not so visible. It's hard to see which parts are important until years later. Or maybe never."

I see her watch me skeptically, and gird myself.

"When I came here, I was so taken by everything that was

different, full of drama, so distinctly Japanese. Like you when you go to America. Now I see it's in the spaces where nothing is happening that one has to make a life."

"Little no-action movie," she says, visibly unpersuaded, and closing the pages of this book without needing to open them. "Rain come down window. Car stuck in traffic jam. Quiet music playing. Autumn light."

Exactly.

Almost the last time we took my father-in-law for a birthday drive—on his final birthday but one—the day dawned cloudless and warm again, a late-October morning like the one that had pierced me on my first day here, thirty years ago, in Narita. Mild and brisk in equal measure: "Come on out," the blue sky said, "but don't expect me to be around for long."

As we drove along the Kamo River, my mother-in-law broke into song. "Oh, I'm so happy," she said to everyone and no one. "It's so good to have a long life. We're going to live to be a hundred!

"You're ninety now," she said to her husband, sleepy and ashen beside her, and he flashed a shy boy's grin, so happy after all these decades to be the object of his wife's affection.

We turned off the main roads and onto the narrow lane that wends its way around sharp turns to Mount Hiei, the haunt of demons—and ferocious soldier monks—overlooking the modern city. Stopping at a 7-Eleven, we bought a picnic of green tea and rice balls and gobbled it down in the parking lot; soon we were in the bracing quiet of the mountain, where monks walk through the night in threadbare sandals, and the thick boom of a temple bell was resounding between the trees as we snaked through the emptiness of the early-autumn afternoon.

Halfway up, we came to a lookout point, completely deserted, with a long wooden board on one side, and a rusty green metered pair of binoculars on the other. Hiroko's father had always wanted to be a teacher, so I encourage him to come and explain the board to me, the history of the mountain. Hiroko's mother sits down on the bright-blue bench, smiles in the brilliant sunshine.

Then Hiroko takes a hundred-yen coin out of her purse and urges her father towards the lookout post. Neither of us has forgotten his delight in purchasing costly binoculars his first afternoon in California; scouting the distance might be his way of returning to the most memorable days of his life, at war.

"Grandpa, step up here," she says, and eases him up by the arm onto a stone, placed there to allow children to peer through the lens. When she puts in the coin, the small figure silently swivels the old instrument from right to left and then, very slowly, from left to right, scanning the horizon.

A silver sliver far below, making a "V" with another river, which it meets. Thick foliage everywhere else, the first touch of yellow and red at its top. A huge expanse with no sign of human habitation; the young man reborn moves the glasses back again from left to right, scanning, scanning.

Behind him, his wife is taking in the sun; Hiroko is delighting in her parents' calm. The cover on the lens is meant to flip down after a minute or two, but it's so ancient, perhaps, it never closes; her father might be looking out for enemy troop movement—for signs of autumn—miles away.

"You're lucky, Grandpa," she sings out. "God is giving you a present. You've been a good man, worked so hard. Now you get a prize!"

He doesn't say a word, as his daughter rubs his shoulders in encouragement, the way I saw her rub her seven-year-old son's shoulders soon after we met. From the back, I see only his sharp jacket and creased trousers; no sign of the rheumy eyes, the teeth now jagged and brown.

"Please enjoy," she goes on. "You have special chance. You don't need stop looking. Ever."

I glance at Hiroko's watch; later this afternoon, I'll have to drop the aging couple at their home, and take the rented car to Kyoto Station. Then a six-hour trip, via a series of bullet trains, up to a broken little town in Fukushima, where a nuclear plant melted down after the tsunami seven months ago.

A war photographer is waiting for me there, and we're going to talk to some of the workers who are risking their lives to go into the poisoned area to try to repair the plant, and ask them why they're doing it. How learn to live with what you can never control?

For now, though, there's nowhere to go on the silent moun-

tain, and a boy who's just turned ninety is surveying the landscape with the rapt eagerness of an Eagle Scout, while his wife
of sixty years sings, "We're so lucky to have a long life!"

Hold this moment forever, I tell myself; it may never come
again.

ACKNOWLEDGMENTS

My first thanks must go to my lifelong adversary and boss, Time, for allowing me, over sixteen years, to sift through an hourly mounting pile of impressions and experiences and feelings, and for showing me, finally, how many of them were useless, or temporary at least. My official bosses at *Time* magazine supported me for many years, and I can never thank them enough for that; but it's Father Time himself who sometimes seems the most bracing editor, even as his reward (as with most editors) is to receive curses around the clock.

On a more day-to-day level, the reader can thank my long-time editor at Knopf, Dan Frank, for the fact that this story isn't weighed down with pages—and more pages—on Wallace Stevens. I grew used, as I was surfacing from a watching of Wimbledon, to receiving engaged and probing messages from Dan even on a Sunday morning, bringing me back to earth and a stronger, better self. Betsy Sallee, in the same office, who helped me in so many ways over the years, offered me the great blessing of her own reading and suggestions for this work, and Terry Zaroff-

Evans graced me with a reassuring and very light copy edit. The pièce de resistance came with a radiant cover designed by Carol Devine Carson (who designed the cover of a book set in Japan I published in 1991) and Abby Weintraub, the intuitive genius who's worked on seven covers for me over nineteen years.

It's a luxury beyond measure, in truth, to be attached to a publishing house where so many of the same encouraging faces have been greeting me for more than three decades now. I can never thank enough Sonny Mehta, Robin Desser, Nicholas Latimer, Kathy Zuckerman and Kate Runde, among many others, who make the creation of books seem such a warm adventure.

In recent years, my life has also been quite wonderfully transformed by the wisdom of the prodigiously resourceful and attentive Miriam Feuerle and her unfailingly friendly and patient crew—Andrew, Hannah, Abigail, Eira and Paige—at the Lyceum Agency. My old friend Lynn Nesbit, together with her colleagues at Janklow & Nesbit Associates, has been keeping me afloat for almost half a lifetime now. In this instance it was Lynn who had the sense to urge me to stop dawdling and start writing again.

I owe a constant debt, too, to those buddies who are always, with a chuckle and a prompt, ready to hold me up to higher standards: Richard Rodriguez and Nicolas Rothwell and Ngari Rinpoche—unlikely trio!—all of whom are brilliant enough to see the limits of brilliance and kind enough to be unsparing in their urging of something a bit beneath the surface.

For quite a while now, my life has been made infinitely warmer and more collegial thanks to the unceasing kindness of Jim and Lynne Doti at Chapman University, such perfect (and irresistible) hosts and friends; and I owe daily thanks from my digital self to the incomparably fun and stylish David Tang and Jeff Cheong at DDB Singapore, and all their cohorts and families, whose generosity humbles, when it isn't inspiring me.

Michael Hofmann has for thirty years been enduring my effusions about Japan, and gently, almost inaudibly, reminding me that there may be more things going on than I can see. He was the only nonprofessional reader I turned to for counsel on this work, and he promptly opened up new horizons with subtlety and tact, much as he'd been opening me out, with quiet care, for several lifetimes.

I'm forever in the debt of the extravagantly spacious—and dangerously addictive—Banff Centre for Arts and Creativity, a place so inspiring it could move a moose to compose sonnets or an Iyer to write symphonies. Is it any wonder that Canada, so generous when it comes to supporting the arts, is also a world leader when it comes to creating community, fashioning a global vision and nurturing an expansive vision of humanity?

It must be obvious from this book how much I owe my neighbors and friends around Shikanodai, in suburban Nara, as well as those (especially the never-complaining Susana Ortiz and Erika Chavez, the saintly Christine and Carl Nolt) who take such loving care of my mother while I'm away. Hiroko Takeuchi and her family have been bringing light and fun to my life for more than half its duration now, and it was the late Keido Fukushima-roshi who brought us all together; this is not a sequel to the book I wrote on Japan twenty-eight years ago, except insofar as autumn is a sequel—a prequel—to spring, the companion piece that rounds the picture out.

I'm very grateful, too, as of this writing, that our daughter is married, to a highly supportive-seeming Japanese Hanshin Tiger fan, and that most of the elderly people I describe in this book are going strong, in their way—even as autumn keeps turning the pages with a dryish smile.

Quite often I'll sit on our tiny terrace, nibbling at sweet tangerines under a high, deep-blue sky, a cup of tea and a novel beside me in the busy quiet, and wonder what I did (or didn't do) to deserve such blessings.

A NOTE ON THE TYPE

Pierre Simon Fournier *le jeune* designed the type used in
this book. He was both an originator and a collector of types.
His services to the art of printing were his design of letters, his
creation of ornaments and initials, and his standardization of type
sizes. In 1764 and 1766 he published his *Manuel typographique,*
and made what many consider his most important contribution to
typography—the measurement of type by the point system.

TYPESET BY SCRIBE, PHILADELPHIA, PENNSYLVANIA
PRINTED AND BOUND BY LSC, HARRISONBURG, VIRGINIA
DESIGNED BY IRIS WEINSTEIN